The Journey of a Postal Employee

Going Postal

BY

Sir Francis T. Blackwood

ISBN: 979-8-3493-7753-2

Table of Contents

CHAPTER 1

Echoes Of Rage

The USPS Plantation was filled with tension. An evil energy hung in the air, like a thick fog that clung to your skin. In the shadows of this government building, a storm was brewing. It was a storm that would soon erupt and shake the very foundations of the Postal Service, an institution haunted by its past.

The first shots rang out on a warm March Day in Tukwila, Washington. They shattered the routine of the mail sorting process. A postal worker, his face twisted in rage, opened fire on a coworker. The body fell to the floor, lifeless. The shooter vanished into the chaos, leaving behind unanswered questions and broken lives.

Just a few months later, the sounds of that violence echoed through the halls of the South Houston Distribution Center in Missouri City, Texas. The crack of gunfire pierced the air again as a disgruntled worker turned his gun on his supervisor. Another life was taken in an instant. This time, the shooter was caught, but the damage was done. The ghosts of the past had returned, refusing to be silenced.

These were not isolated incidents. They were the latest chapters in a dark and troubled history that had long plagued the United States Postal Service. For decades, the organization had been scarred by workplace shootings. Each one was a testament to the deep pain and unresolved conflicts that festered within.

From Los Angeles to Alabama, the names of the victims had become a litany of sorrow - Harry Sendrow, Curtis Collins, James Brooks, Steven Brownlee. And looming above them all was the specter of Patrick Sherrill, whose rampage in Edmond, Oklahoma, became the deadliest in postal history, a grim milestone that would echo through the years.

These were not just names on a page. They were human beings - fathers, mothers, brothers, sisters. Their lives were snuffed out in a blaze of violence, a product of a system that had failed them. As the smoke cleared, the haunting question remained: how did it come to this?

The answers seemed to lie buried within the USPS Plantation, a microcosm of the organization's problems, where the ghosts of the past continued to haunt the present. It was here, amidst the chaos and disorder, that one employee would embark on a journey to uncover the truth, to shed light on the darkness that had consumed so many before.

For in the shadows of the USPS Plantation, a reckoning was coming. It would test the limits of human endurance and challenge the very foundations of an institution that had lost its way. The echoes of rage would not be silenced, not this time. The time for change had arrived, and the battle lines had been drawn.

CHAPTER 2

Formative Journey

They say our past helps shape our future. As I close my eyes and dive into some deep thoughts, I can't help but reflect on the journey that has brought me to this point.

As a child, I was naturally introverted, often finding solace in my own company even as I had friends around me. In a room filled with many people, I would remain silent unless someone made an effort to engage me. My older brother, who was a year my senior, was the polar opposite - far more social and outgoing, often speaking for both of us.

In school, the contrast between my brother and I was stark. While he excelled academically, I struggled. When we began learning to read, my father would try to teach us, but every time he pointed to a letter, it felt as if my brain had been scrambled. I simply couldn't identify the letters easily, and this often resulted in punishment. I hated feeling inferior to my brother, and I sensed my father's preference for him.

Due to these academic challenges, I became withdrawn at a young age. I started to doubt my own worth, especially when compared to my brother and the other children my father held up as examples. Imagine being a child, watching others praise your sibling's intelligence while you are labeled as "dumb." It was a heavy burden to bear. The punishment I would receive for not knowing the answers only exacerbated my anxiety, leading to panic attacks whenever I was called on in class.

However, I discovered that I had a unique talent - the ability to easily grasp and mimic physical skills. I would observe my uncles playing soccer, meticulously studying their movements, and then replay the actions in my mind until I could execute them flawlessly. This talent manifested in various ways, from quickly learning to swim after observing others to mastering complex dive and gymnastics techniques.

While I excelled at physical activities, academics were a constant struggle. I hated going to school, dreading the moments when teachers would call on me. I found myself staring out the window, disconnected from the lessons rather than engaging. My poor performance in school led my father to believe I was lazy, and he resorted to punishment in an attempt to motivate me.

In hindsight, I now recognize the possibility of learning disorders like dyslexia or ADHD, but my father dismissed these as excuses. His belief that I was simply being "lazy" only exacerbated the problem, leading to panic attacks whenever I was asked to read or participate in class.

As I progressed through school, my academic struggles continued while my athletic prowess grew. I found solace in sports, excelling in soccer and earning the attention of coaches who recruited me for tournaments. However, my father's demands that I focus on my studies led him to eventually ban me from participating in these activities.

The loss of my athletic outlets plunged me into a deep depression, and I began to surround myself with the wrong crowd, skipping school and nearly failing to graduate. It was a tumultuous time, filled with challenges that strained my relationship with my family and threatened to derail my future.

Yet, through it all, I maintained a glimmer of hope. After begging my way back into school and eventually graduating, I embarked on a journey of self-discovery at the university level. However, even there, I struggled to find my footing, jumping from one major to the next as I grappled with my passions and identity.

It was during this time that I met my wife, and we started a family together. I found stability in a career as a night audit supervisor, but the desire to pursue my true passion, filmmaking, never waned. Just as I was making progress in that direction, the COVID-19 pandemic disrupted my plans, leading to the dissolution of my marriage.

As I reflect on this winding path, I can't help but feel a sense of both pride and trepidation. The challenges I've faced have shaped me in profound ways, and yet, I find myself once again searching for that elusive direction. But this time, with the lessons of the past etched into my being, I can't help but feel a glimmer of hope that perhaps this new journey at the USPS will lead me to my purpose. I don't know why I am here, but I trust that there's a reason, and I am optimistic.

CHAPTER 3

Going Postal

We have all heard the phrase "going postal." What does that phrase mean to you? How does it make you feel when you hear it?

For those who don't know, "going postal" is an American English slang phrase that refers to becoming extremely and uncontrollably angry, often to the point of violence, usually in a workplace environment. The expression derives from a series of incidents beginning in 1986, in which United States Postal Service (USPS) workers shot and killed managers, fellow workers, police officers, and members of the general public in acts of mass murder.

The most notorious of these incidents occurred on August 20, 1986, in Edmond, Oklahoma, when a postal worker named Patrick Henry Sherrill entered his workplace armed with several guns and unleashed a deadly rampage on his coworkers.

However, the tragic history of postal shootings did not begin or end with the Edmond incident. In December 1983, in Anniston, Alabama, a postal worker named

James Brooks entered the post office with a .38 -caliber pistol, killing the postmaster and then pursuing his supervisor up the stairs, shooting him twice and injuring him.

Initially, when I heard about people "going postal," I didn't understand it. I thought it was simply people acting irrationally. However, after working at the USPS Plantation for nearly five years, I now understand how someone could be pushed to the point of reacting out of anger when they feel unheard, and their issues remain unresolved.

This realization motivates me to write this book. I recognize that not everyone can channel their struggles into making a difference. Some may take their anger and react violently, leading to headlines like "USPS Employee Goes Postal." Was that person truly insane, or were they pushed to their limit, feeling they had no resources or help available to them?

As I embark on this journey, I can't help but wonder how many others have found themselves in a similar predicament, trapped in a workplace that seems to prioritize profits over the well-being of its employees.

CHAPTER 4

Walk with Me

In our neighborhoods, the mail carrier is a familiar sight, often overlooked. They walk the streets, sorting through piles of letters meant for the next mailbox, bringing a sense of connection to the community. In pleasant neighborhoods, you might see a mail carrier smiling and waving at neighbors, spreading cheer like the festive spirit of a New York Christmas parade. Here, they seem happy, as if they expect a little gratitude from the people they serve, the letter writers. Good customer service is just part of life in these areas.

However, the atmosphere changes in tougher neighborhoods. There, you might find your mail carrier wearing headphones and talking loudly on the phone while sorting mail. This behavior reflects their unease; staying on the phone helps them feel safer, signaling to anyone nearby that they are not alone. They often avoid eye contact to steer clear of trouble. In these places, the reality is harsh, where people may be more likely to pull triggers than to write letters, transforming the simple act of delivering mail into a risky task.

As you step into the shadows of the postal system, the familiar cheer and warmth of the neighborhood mail carrier fade, replaced by an ominous atmosphere that seeps into the walls of the facility. The floors, once polished and gleaming, now bear the scars of neglect, their dusty surfaces a testament to the indifference that permeates this place. The air itself carries a weight, tainted by the acrid stench of diesel fuel, a pungent reminder of the industrial nature of this environment. Voices echo through the hallways, not in the joyful cadence of greeting but in the discordant symphony of anger, frustration, and despair.

This story is not one of the familiar, friendly mail carriers but a descent into the very heart of the postal system, where the light of hope seems to flicker and fade, replaced by the unsettling realization that something sinister lurks beneath the surface. Welcome to the dungeon, the USPS Plantation, where the rules of the outside world no longer apply, and the very foundations of justice and humanity are tested to their limits.

CHAPTER 5

Entering the World of Mail Handling

During the peak of the COVID-19 pandemic, I applied to many different places for employment. While I was doing a lot of freelance work, the pandemic significantly impacted business. Then, I received a call from a company that had a contract with the prison system in the area. I went through the entire background check process before receiving the green light to start working with this company. Passing the background check granted me access to the prison to do my job.

While working in the correctional facilities, I began to build relationships with some of the guards there. During one conversation, the topic of wages came up, and the amount the guard mentioned he made last year surprised me. He then said something that got me thinking: “If you’re able to come in here, that means you passed a rigorous background check. Why are you doing this job when you could work here as a correctional officer and earn a lot more money with all this unlimited overtime we have?”

I went home that day and started applying for correctional officer positions and some government jobs since I had already passed such a rigorous background check. I received a letter inviting me for an interview for a correctional officer position. Before I knew it, I was in the process of completing the background check to become a correctional officer. When I informed my family about my decision, they were not pleased and were concerned about the dangers of working closely with dangerous individuals during COVID. One family member even mentioned a news report discussing how many inmates in the jail and prison systems were dying from COVID-19 and how it was spreading like wildfire.

That explained why the correctional officers had unlimited overtime; no one wanted to come to work due to the risk of catching COVID. However, the money was so enticing that I was still eager to pursue becoming a correctional officer. The next day, while checking my mail, I received a letter from the Postal Service. Within about a week or two, I went through the entire new hire process with the Postal Service, attended orientation, and was pleased with what I heard and saw in the videos they showed us.

One thing that truly convinced me to take the job was the fact that this would make me a government worker. Government employees receive excellent benefits, which I wanted due to the COVID situation. If I had good insurance and contracted COVID, I could survive; that was my mindset. I won't lie; I was very happy to be a government worker. From the outside looking in, I had the impression that working as a postal employee would be something like the commercials you see during the Christmas season, featuring mail carriers smiling, waving, and playing with dogs while greeting neighbors.

CHAPTER 6

Welcome to The Devil's Playground - USPS Plantation

Today was my first day at the USPS Plantation (the name used to refer to the postal facility). It was 9:30 PM, and the facility was about an hour from my home. My shift was set to start at 10:00 PM and end at 6:30 AM. I was well aware that an overnight job can negatively impact mental health, cause digestive issues and sleep disorders, and increase the risk of accidents, mood changes, vitamin D deficiency, and other health concerns. Yet, I remained hopeful and excited to start this new chapter.

I entered the address into my GPS and began driving towards the USPS Plantation. When my GPS indicated I had arrived, I looked at my surroundings, confused. All I saw were trailers parked in the lot. However, using common sense and knowing that GPS can sometimes mislead when it comes to large property entrances, I decided to drive around.

I made my way to the other side of the property and came across a parking lot resembling a dealership's lot. I automatically knew that it must be the employee parking lot. As I got closer, I noticed a small line of cars entering the parking lot, and upon closer inspection, I saw a barrier that raised as cars passed through, only to come back down afterward.

Not long after, I found myself in line as the barrier continued to rise and drop. When it was my turn, the barrier dropped in front of me. I looked to my left and saw a small box with a card reader, realizing I did not have access to enter the employee parking lot. I searched for a button to contact someone inside to let me in, but I didn't see any. Headlights began lining up behind me, and the drivers were not too happy, responding with honks and urging me to move. To exit, everyone had to reverse to let me out. I eventually managed to reverse and park my car on the street, then made my way up the small hill leading to the main entrance doors.

Upon reaching the entrance, I pulled out one of the double glass doors. After taking just a couple of steps, I began to feel a prison-like atmosphere due to the rotating black metal gate. I pushed the metal rotating gate to enter the building, but it did not budge. That's when someone behind me said, "You need a badge to get in," pointing at the intercom with a camera. I pressed the button, and it rang, but no one answered. After a few minutes, someone asked if I was new. I told them yes, and they invited me in, swiping their badge for entry. I followed as the metal door spun, letting us through to the other side.

I was officially in the building. Straight ahead, through a long, airy hallway, was a cafeteria resembling a prison cafeteria with bench tables. I felt a little institutionalized as I walked toward this area. "Excuse me, do you know where the main office is? I don't know where to go," I asked the young lady who had let me in.

"Yes," she replied. "Go straight; after you pass the vending machine, make a right, then your next left. You will see a door to your left; that's the general clerk's office."

"I said the main office, not the general clerk's office," I corrected her.

"The general clerk's office is our main office," she explained.

"Thank you," I replied, following her instructions. I stood there and knocked for a few minutes until someone behind me asked if I was new. I confirmed I was, and they told me to have a seat in the cafeteria. I sat there for a few moments as the seats around me began to fill with other new employees. Soon, a lady entered and announced that all new employees should follow her. We all got up like fresh recruits and followed her into a room where someone had set up an old 1949-style TV. The video was so outdated that I could have sworn it was shot in the '70s or '80s, at the latest, the early '90s.

This video explained the proper ways to handle mail and use equipment. I hate sitting still for too long, so I asked how long the process would take. They said not too long, and about 30 minutes later, we all got up and toured the property, where the HR lady introduced different operations and where each person would be working.

As we toured the building, I noticed a large volume of mail scattered everywhere, with barely any space to store more. I also observed many employees were not actually working; instead, they were engaged in personal conversations. The language I heard shocked me; considering it was a government job, I assumed everyone would be more professional. I quickly realized there was no organization in how the mail was being moved. Everything was chaotic, and many people looked confused about their tasks.

Eventually, two other new hires and I were told we would likely be working in the Platform B Section (different areas/operations within the Platform). After the orientation and building tour, along with some paperwork, we went to our assigned operation. When we arrived, we were confused because no one was there to train us. So, we decided to observe what other workers were doing, following their lead until we received further instructions from a supervisor or manager.

As time went on, it was almost 6:30 AM, and it was time to clock out. I started to reflect on the night and realized the postal service job was nothing like I had expected. I guess I had higher hopes. I was truly let down.

CHAPTER 7

Getting Acclimated at The Plantation

The next day, I returned to work, and this time, my two new colleagues and I were introduced to an elderly gentleman named Mr. Mumbles, who served as the Platform (the central sorting/loading area) team lead. Understanding him proved to be quite challenging; he mumbled and spoke in a very low tone. Despite his efforts to train us, it was evident that he had been on the job for a long time and lacked enthusiasm. He definitely seemed ready for retirement, looking worn out and frequently dozing off. I couldn't blame him; his age certainly took its toll.

We were also introduced to a Caucasian man, the expediter (a worker who coordinates mail movement) for Section B, whom I'll refer to as Mr. Slick. As the story unfolds, you'll understand why I chose that name. Mr Slick had oddly colored hair and gave off the impression of being an ex-meth addict. Fortunately, my work buddies and I got along well and worked efficiently together. Management appreciated our ability to complete tasks quickly, and over time, we became the go-to people when things needed to get done. Before long, we learned to operate various equipment, including double forks, forklifts, and OX machines (all types of equipment used for moving mail). With these skills, management sought us out for help, knowing we were hard workers who got the job done. Our efforts didn't go unnoticed; everyone in the building knew our names because of our dedication. Some managers even began to make deals with us, offering incentives like extra breaks in exchange for our assistance in clearing the floor. We loved those deals and felt like rock stars in the USPS Plantation.

The transition from having no supervisor at the Platform to being ordered around by a woman I nicknamed Prada was quite a shock. At first, I didn't like her, and I sensed she didn't care for me either. However, as time went on, we grew closer and began discussing personal matters over the phone. Our conversations lasted for over an hour, and a mutual attraction developed between us. One day, I was supposed to meet her at an event but ended up canceling at the last minute. She was already at the event, tipsy and waiting for me, which understandably upset her. My failure to show up caused our personal relationship to wane. What I truly appreciated about her was her feistiness, and she was undeniably attractive with flawless skin, clearly taking great care of herself.

CHAPTER 8

USPS Plantation is Going Downhill

Within about a year, things began to change significantly. Mr. Mumbles retired, and in his place, they hired a young lady whom I nicknamed 34x34. She earned this nickname because she wore clothes that didn't fit her properly, particularly her jeans, which she folded over several times to avoid dragging on the floor. I wear size 34 by 34, and it can be challenging to find that size in stores, especially when someone else is taking up sizes that don't suit them, making it even harder for those who genuinely need size 34 by 34.

34x34's work ethic was lacking; she was known for being lazy and often vanished when it was time to work. Despite this, she was appointed as the Platform team lead. The decision to promote her wasn't well thought out, as the system USPS uses for filling positions does not prioritize hiring the best candidates. Essentially, when a position opens up, employees bid on it, and those with seniority usually get the job. As a result, many people occupy roles for which they are not qualified and should never have been considered.

Soon after, many changes swept through the workplace: new supervisors and new MDOs. The biggest mistake they made was promoting a woman I nicknamed Lips to an MDO. Lips was very unattractive and had a peculiar body shape, reminiscent of a linebacker with broad shoulders and a strong, muscular neck. She wore high-heeled wedges and stomped heavily on the cement floor as she walked. Lips was an untrained, aggressive manager who terrorized everyone, including the supervisors. I nicknamed her Lips because she frequently licked her lips when she looked at me. She often stood behind me while I worked, making strange noises; whatever sound you might imagine a very large person makes when they see a chocolate cake is akin to the noise she made while standing near me.

Another reason I called her Lips is that one day, while I was driving equipment, she looked me dead in the eyes and placed one leg on top of stacked pallets as if she intended to show me something inappropriate. As soon as another employee approached with their equipment, Lips quickly closed her legs. It's worth mentioning that she was wearing a skirt, which made it clear she wanted to reveal something I did not want to see. I found her unattractive and wished she would keep her legs closed.

I've heard rumors about her and how people speculate she obtained her management role. I heard she was married but still had affairs with married men, and she was even caught having sex inside a truck with a truck driver. Additionally, 34x34 informed me that Lips had an interest in me, and others confirmed this as well. However,

I was not interested at all. The workplace was already chaotic, but with the introduction of new, untrained people in managerial positions, it became unbearable. The work environment deteriorated to the point that two of my close work buddies left to find jobs elsewhere. With the pressure now resting heavily on me, I started calling off frequently.

CHAPTER 9

I'm Back!

After frequently calling off, I decided it was time to return to work regularly. Upon my return, I noticed some new faces in the B section of the Platform. One of them was a young lady who had previously worked at a different operation but had now been transferred to our section. The story behind her transfer was that Lips, an MDO, didn't like her. Since the B section is the most physically demanding area in the entire building, Lips seemed to view this as a form of punishment for the young lady, whom I would call Gothic. Gothic had a very dark, brooding aura about her; she barely spoke and never made eye contact; her gaze perpetually fixed on the scuffed concrete floor as she moved about with an almost defensive posture. I noticed she almost exclusively wore black clothing. She would sometimes walk around staring intently at her phone, using it as a barrier to avoid any potential interaction with her coworkers. She arrived early and left early, ensuring minimal contact with the others during her shifts, and took her breaks in isolated corners of the building as if she were actively trying to make herself invisible.

We also had a new male coworker who didn't say much, either. Dan was a tall, muscular-built guy with a long mop of shaggy brown hair sprinkled with grays and a perpetual five o'clock shadow also streaked with gray. His movements were deliberate, and he carried himself with a relaxed, almost casual air as he went about his work. Since the three of us were quiet and focused primarily on our tasks, it made it easier for us to get things done efficiently. We worked so well together that we didn't need to verbalize our needs to accomplish our duties - a nod here, a subtle hand gesture there, and we were in sync.

Having worked alongside Mr Slick for over a year, I began to notice changes in his behavior. The first thing that stood out to me was his manipulation skills. With many of the supervisors and MDOs being new and not properly trained, they would often turn to Mr. Slick for guidance, given his 25 years of experience. He would greet them with a wide, toothy grin and a hearty laugh, but during our smoke breaks, I would observe his expression shift, his lips curling into a knowing smirk as he spoke disparagingly about the very same managers, he had just been charming. This inconsistency made me distrust him - I could sense the gears turning in his mind, calculating his next move.

As a dog lover who has owned several pups in my lifetime, I understand how excited they can get when I come home. However, Mr. Slick shared a story about how his dogs would actually run away from him when he arrived home, cowering and whimpering. He also mentioned that his disabled wife somehow always seemed to be falling down the steps, an oddly specific detail that set off alarm bells in my mind. His stepdaughter, he revealed, wanted nothing to do with him, and he even admitted to having her fired without her knowing he was responsible. I could almost see the manipulation dripping from his words, and I knew not to trust a single thing that came out of his mouth. Those who gossip with you will eventually gossip about you, which is why I chose to listen rather than engage in conversation.

One day, while smoking, he removed his dentures and shared his past as a drug addict, explaining his rough appearance. His use of meth and other hard drugs left him with leathery skin and jittery movements. I noticed he began handling mail, which was against union rules for clerks. He also redirected me to less important tasks while helping unload trucks himself, slowing down our process. His interference confused me.

CHAPTER 10

Lips is So Unprofessional

I'll never forget my first major confrontation with Lips. Management had always made special arrangements with my crew and me, understanding that my intense work ethic meant I needed proper rest. My previous MDO respected that I hadn't signed up for overtime, so we'd agreed I'd work shorter shifts on my off days. Every manager knew about this arrangement - except Lips.

Her reaction to my early departure - after completing my agreed-upon four hours - revealed her true character. My contributions were significant; everyone noticed when I wasn't there. Word spread quickly about my departure, and Lips's response was telling. The next morning, as soon as I entered the building, the whispers began. "Lips is furious with you," someone called out. Another employee explained she was upset about my early departure. "I'll address it with her directly," I replied calmly.

By the time clock, another coworker warned me about an impending write-up. Her unprofessional behavior - discussing my situation with everyone except me - was particularly galling. The gossip followed me to the B section of the Platform, where I finally encountered Lips herself. I confronted the situation head-on: "I understand you're upset about yesterday. I worked the hours agreed upon with management." I emphasized how inappropriately she'd handled the situation, spreading my personal business before speaking with me.

Like an untrained pitbull, she erupted into a public display of authority, yelling across the Platform. Her behavior pushed me to the edge of my composure, but I maintained control. When she demanded to see me in her office at 6:25 AM, she likely expected intimidation. Instead, I had my own agenda - a discussion about professional conduct and confidentiality.

At 6:20 AM, I was already at the general clerk's office, eager to address her unprofessional behavior. The meeting room confrontation revealed her backpedaling: "I was worried about you - thought you might have been kidnapped." My response was measured but firm: "A simple check of the time clock would show I properly clocked out. Unlike others, I don't hide while on the clock. My time records show this same pattern every weekend - approved by other MDOs and supervisors. If policies changed, no one informed me. I've been honoring an agreement made when I declined overtime, doing this as a courtesy because the previous MDO showed genuine professional leadership."

Though I kept certain thoughts unspoken, my message was clear. As a 6'3", dark-skinned, 215-pound Black man, I'm acutely aware that raising my voice could trigger unfair stereotypes. Instead, I let my professionalism speak volumes.

CHAPTER 11

Mr. Slick Turns into a Stalker

I worked in the B section of the Platform as the main equipment driver. My job was to move mail around using machines like double forks, oxen, and forklifts. I was always busy, so I rarely talked with my coworkers, Dan and Gothic.

When Gothic first started working with us, I didn't think she would last long. She wasn't very big - maybe 150 to 170 pounds - and our work was really physical. Many people had quit because it was too hard. But I was wrong about Gothic. She worked harder than most of the men who came through our section.

One day, I asked Dan, "How does she keep up this energy all night?" Dan just said that's how she was. I kept thinking about this while driving my equipment.

After a few months, I started noticing something strange. Mr. Slick would always show up when Dan and Gothic were unloading trucks. During our busiest times, when we needed everyone's help, he would send Gothic to do less important tasks. I asked Dan about this, and he told me Mr. Slick was giving Gothic different jobs to do - even though Mr. Slick wasn't even a supervisor.

Mr. Slick kept finding ways to work near Gothic, pulling her away from important work to do things that could wait. This bothered me, but since Gothic and I didn't talk, I kept quiet.

Everything changed during one late-night smoke break. I saw Gothic vaping alone. After working together for six months without talking, it seemed weird to stay silent. When we finally talked, I was surprised by how well-spoken she was - different from the usual loud workplace chatter.

We ended up exchanging phone numbers. I did it my usual way - writing my number on paper and passing it to her quietly. As we talked more on the phone, we found out we had a lot in common. I loved writing, and she loved reading. She spoke so well because she read a lot, but most people didn't know this because she was so quiet.

While we kept our friendship secret at work, Gothic told me something important: Mr. Slick had feelings for her. This explained why he kept following her around the building, even though his job didn't require him to.

Things got worse when Mr. Slick changed Gothic's work schedule to match his. She used to work 10 PM to 6:30 AM, but he made it 11 PM to 7:30 AM - just like his hours. This left me working alone during our busiest time, so management had to change her schedule back. Gothic told me she had only accepted one ride from Mr Slick when he saw her at a bus stop and that he had made her uncomfortable by calling her beautiful.

We realized Mr. Slick changed her schedule so he could offer her rides more often. Gothic asked me to talk to him about his behavior. When I did, he apologized and promised to stop. He even apologized to Gothic directly, and she told him clearly to leave her alone so she could work. We thought that would fix things, but it didn't.

Then Mr. Slick started worrying about Gothic and Dan's friendship. He noticed Dan gave her rides, but she refused his offers. Soon after, Dan was moved to a different section. Mr. Slick told me Dan had asked to move, but when I talked to Dan, he said that wasn't true - he loved working with us.

With Dan gone, Mr. Slick started up again. He even got management to keep me busy away from the B section. Things got creepy when he mentioned seeing Gothic with her kids. This really worried her.

When a new guy nicknamed Mushroom joined our section, the same thing happened. As soon as he started talking to Gothic, Mr. Slick got angry, saying, "This isn't a dating show!" I warned Mushroom he'd get moved if he kept talking to Gothic. He didn't listen, and sure enough, he was soon transferred out.

Through all of this, Gothic and I had become close friends, but nobody knew. We kept it secret until our matching break times gave us away. Finally, Mr. Slick figured out that I - not Dan or Mushroom - was the one who had gotten close to Gothic.

CHAPTER 12

Cat and Mouse Game (Tom & Jerry)

Mr. Slick started acting really strangely in the Gothic genre. He would hide behind equipment just to watch her. Gothic, and I knew we had to do something about it. We told him straight up that we didn't need his help with the trucks anymore and reminded him that his job was just to be an expediter - that's what his union contract said. He didn't like it, but he knew Gothic could report him to the bosses if he didn't stop.

Whenever I was busy driving equipment and delivering mail, Mr. Slick would try to get close to Gothic. He'd hang around her work area and makeup reasons to talk to her when I wasn't there. We figured out how to handle this - I'd either come back quickly, or Gothic would walk over to where I was working. This made him back off. Things got more tense when he saw Gothic and me going to lunch together. You could tell he was suspicious about us.

His behavior got worse. He started timing his movements to match Gothic movements. He'd wait by the doors and bump into her like it was an accident. Gothic knew these weren't really accidents. I kept watching him carefully because I didn't trust what he might do. I worried he might try to cause trouble for me at work.

I started changing my mail delivery routes to throw him off. This really frustrated him - you could see him getting angry when he couldn't figure out where I'd be. He'd walk back and forth, trying to keep track of both Gothic and me. Gothic and I sometimes laughed about how ridiculous it all was, but we knew his behavior was getting out of hand.

This went on for months, with just the three of us knowing what was really happening. Mr. Slick tried a new trick - he'd talk to anyone standing near Gothic while secretly watching us. We decided to talk to a coworker we called Ellen DeGeneres (because she looked like a famous comedian). Ellen had worked there for over 20 years, so we thought she might know what to do.

Ellen thought we should talk to the union about it, but Gothic didn't want to make things bigger. Instead, Ellen helped by watching Mr. Slick herself and eventually told him to stop. He behaved better for a little while but soon went back to his old ways. He was just more careful about it now because he knew Ellen was watching.

CHAPTER 13

The Over-thinker Side of Me

I kept wondering about Mr. Slick's obsession with Gothic. It didn't make sense - here was a married man acting like a lovesick teenager. He seemed convinced there was something special between them, but based on what? The more I watched his behavior, the more confused I became.

I decided to talk to Gothic directly about it. I needed to know if there was anything in their past that might explain his fixation. Had they ever been involved? Was there some connection I didn't know about? Gothic was clear and firm - there had never been anything between them. Not even close.

This made Mr Slick's behavior even more disturbing. He was living in some kind of fantasy world, completely disconnected from reality. He acted like he and Gothic shared a secret romance when, in truth, she barely acknowledged his existence. While I knew I needed to stay alert and protect Gothic from his unwanted attention, I couldn't help but wonder what was going on in his mind. What made him create this imaginary relationship, and why couldn't he accept the truth?

CHAPTER 14

Mr. Slick Unleashes the Wolf Pack on Gothic and Me

Mr. Slick's hatred for me had reached a boiling point. I even joked to Gothic that if he ever snapped, I'd probably be his first target. He launched a smear campaign, starting with truck drivers, then moving to coworkers, and finally reaching management. I noticed everyone he talked to would end up staring at me.

I'd learned something important about gossip: watch the listener, not the speaker. The listener always glances at whoever they're talking about. That's exactly what was happening - everyone Mr. Slick spoke to would eventually look my way. The workplace atmosphere changed dramatically. People stopped returning greetings, conversations would die when we walked by, and something felt very wrong.

Soon, supervisors from other departments started watching us work - something they'd never done before. My heightened awareness of my surroundings, which some might call paranoia, picked up on every detail. This sensitivity stemmed from a traumatic childhood experience in Nigeria when I was five.

My brother and I were walking to visit our mother in the hospital after she'd given birth. A pickup truck suddenly pulled up beside us, filled with strangers claiming our mother had sent them. Something felt wrong. When they jumped out to grab us, we ran into the dense woods. We could hear them crashing through the foliage behind us, shouting threats. Stories of children disappearing for ritual sacrifices filled our minds as we hid behind a massive tree, hearts pounding.

We stayed frozen, barely breathing, as they searched. Their voices echoed through the trees, getting closer, then gradually fading away. Only when complete silence returned did we dare move. We survived, but that day left a permanent mark.

This experience shaped my instincts. I notice every change in people's routines and movements. At work, these instincts were now signaling danger. The atmosphere had become charged with whispers and strange energy. Walking to our break area became an exercise in observation. Groups would fall silent as we approached, then burst into loud conversation after we passed. Mr. Slick's influence was spreading.

Frustrated that we wouldn't react to the gossip, Mr. Slick changed tactics. He aligned himself with MDO Lips, the most aggressive supervisor in the building. She ruled with absolute control, forcing even other supervisors to get her approval for basic decisions. The only person who ever stood up to her was Supervisor Prada, who once memorably ordered Lips off her platform. But after Prada moved to a different shift, things got worse.

A new policy requiring supervisor rotation every three months only added to the chaos. New supervisors barely understood their roles before being moved elsewhere. One admitted to me she only grasped 35% of her duties before transferring. This led to constant errors and confusion. During one critical situation with a time-sensitive truck shipment; supervisors wasted precious minutes arguing instead of solving the problem. I had to step in and coordinate the solution myself.

With Prada gone, Lips' control grew stronger. Every new supervisor became her puppet, following her orders without question. Now, with Mr. Slick whispering in her ear, the situation was becoming dangerous. He knew Lips had sent Gothic to the platform as punishment, and he also knew Lips liked me. The thought of Gothic and me together would infuriate her. I could see Lips gathering her allies, preparing for something bigger.

CHAPTER 15

Lips, Puppet Supervisor, Pound Cake

Pound Cake is short and stocky, much like those hefty, loaf-shaped pound cakes. If you have a vivid imagination, you can easily see the resemblance.

She had little knowledge of the platform, and honestly, I doubt they placed her there expecting her to make a positive impact. Nevertheless, being a puppet, she jumped right into her work. I've experienced this scenario countless times; it feels like a routine script they all follow. The first step is usually to instruct you to take on more tasks, knowing that everyone around you is slacking off. They expect you to complete your current work before piling on additional responsibilities.

Then, the issue of breaks arose. Mr. Slick was still upset that Gothic and I had taken our breaks together, so he attempted to call me to drive for a section I wasn't assigned to, the C section. At that time, drivers were designated to specific sections. When break time came, he contacted me, claiming he needed a driver to help with Door

29. Mind you, we worked in the B section, and there was a driver usually sitting right beside him. But he insisted I should do it, fully aware that he wanted to prevent me from going to lunch at the same time as Gothic, leaving me stuck while she went to lunch alone.

I didn't heed his request because he wasn't my supervisor, and that wasn't my section. Additionally, there was someone assigned to that section who could handle it, but he still wanted me to take on the task. Once he realized I wouldn't comply, they devised another plan. The twist was to send the C-section driver on break around the time we usually took our breaks so that Miss Pound Cake could inform me I couldn't go on break. I was utterly confused. What was happening here? Many of these individuals were people I had seniority over. After I refused to play along and went to lunch at my usual time, he became upset, but honestly, I didn't care. They were clearly going to great lengths to make my life miserable.

Not long after, Miss Pound Cake called a platform meeting. During this meeting, she announced that we would be moving people around to allow everyone to learn different sections. The A, B, and C sections each had their own expediters: Mr. Slick for B, Ellen for A, and Ms. Peace for C. Generally, everyone has a specific section they work in daily. Since I started in this facility, I've only worked in the B section, and regulars typically stick to their assigned areas. Mail Handlers Assistants (MHAs) can be moved at any time.

It seemed the Wolf Pack had held a meeting and decided to move everyone around. However, their plan was to shift every single person to a section they had never worked in, except for Gothic. Many were unhappy about this, including Ms. Peace and Ellen, because they were accustomed to their mail handlers and didn't have to train them anymore since they knew their daily tasks. This change only complicated their responsibilities. Being outspoken, I challenged this decision. I requested a meeting with Miss Pound Cake and explained that this move would negatively impact the platform. We were already understaffed, facing closures, and dealing with an influx of mail. This was not the time to switch things around. With the volume of mail we were handling, it was impractical to learn a new section without adequate training resources.

If everyone is moved, who will train whom? The only person remaining stationary is Gothic. I knew the decision was not aimed at improving mail efficiency; it stemmed from personal motives and emotions, not from a desire to benefit the facility.

To illustrate their lack of foresight, I recalled a conversation with a supervisor regarding how much information she retained from her last operation after spending three months there. That supervisor was Miss Pound Cake, and she admitted she retained only 35%. If one can only remember 35% of an operation after three months, imagine the chaos of moving everyone around and expecting the expediters and our team lead, who is often high and asleep in the break area, to train them while dealing with a daily influx of mail.

I conveyed to her that I understood why the expediters were upset, except for Mr. Slick, who orchestrated this plan just as he had arranged for Gothic's schedule to mirror his. When I spoke with Ellen, she immediately expressed her concerns, saying, "I don't think it's fair that Mr. Slick gets to keep Gothic while all the expediters have new people in their sections." After explaining how unreasonable the plan sounded, I informed her that Miss Pound Cake was making these decisions because of Mr. Slick. It became clear that the unnecessary changes were designed to please him, and it was unfair to the other expediters. This situation upset Ellen enough that she initiated a conversation about whether we had reached out to the union representative she had referred us to.

CHAPTER 16

Be a Man

Something happened that caused the driver to be moved from the C-section to the B-section, but now, in the B-section, he no longer drives. It seems he must have done something to end up here, likely after an incident where he was unhappy with how someone spoke to him, leading him to declare, "I'm not driving any equipment anymore." As a form of punishment, they reassigned him to the B-section, the most physically demanding area on the entire property. In this section, workers are forced to pull heavy items over long distances to various operations, often while drivers disappear, leaving management to insist that you physically walk heavy mail wherever they want it delivered.

Even though you know this is wrong and want to refuse, compliance becomes necessary. If you don't go along with it, you risk facing charges like "failure to follow direct orders" or similar nonsense. When management starts throwing around charges like that and using petty tactics, their goal is to get you out of there.

Let's refer to the C-section driver as Mr. Rap-a-Lot. There seems to be some tension between him and 34X34. They appeared to be on good terms before; I don't recall them ever having issues. However, something serious must have happened, and I think I know what it is. Mr. Rap-a-Lot had grown very comfortable with 34X34 to the point where he barely did any work. He could disappear for hours without anyone raising an eyebrow, as 34X34 would only call him when absolutely necessary. He enjoyed a sort of VIP treatment.

Now, Mr. Rap-a-Lot has become conditioned to this lack of responsibility, and he's used to sleeping at certain times. Without the protection of 34X34 and unable to retreat to his car, he continued these habits in the B-section. While in the C-section, he would sleep right on the platform, but after 34X34 raised concerns with management about his behavior, they started to crack down on him. As part of the Wolfpack, 34X34 has the power to set things in motion to get someone in trouble.

One day, things escalated between 34X34 and Mr. Rap-a-Lot. He grew frustrated with feeling picked on and believed everyone was intentionally targeting him. Previously, people would look the other way regarding his actions, but now that he and 34X34 were no longer on good terms, she magnified every little thing he did. This led to an argument during which 34X34 used phrases like "be a man" and "you're not a man," attacking his masculinity.

It struck me as odd that 34X34 would say this to Mr Rap-a-Lot, considering he is a married man with four or five kids, while 34X34 identifies as a masculine lesbian. I'm not sure of the correct terminology, but she embodies the stereotype of a more masculine type of lesbian. Mr. Rap-a-Lot responded with typical angry language, "Fuck you, you're not going to do shit, fuck outta here", while 34X34, who acts like a man, told him to "be a man." Honestly, I thought to myself that she was projecting her own desires; she wished she were a man, which is why she mimics male behaviors.

This was actually the second argument I should mention. The first one I witnessed stemmed from Mr. Rap-a-Lot's conditioned work ethic, which had previously been supported by management and 34X34 before their situation escalated. Once 34X34 made it clear that Mr. Rap-a-Lot was always sleeping, others began to pick on him, and harassment initiated by her took off.

The expediter, whom I nicknamed Mrs. Pastor, usually covers for Mr. Slick when he's off or called out. On this day, she was expediting and was pretty close with 34X34. Out of nowhere, she complained that Mr. Rap-a-Lot wasn't doing anything, prompting 34X34 to come to the B-section. As the argument escalated, 34X34 resorted to gender-based insults, questioning his masculinity and saying all the things that would trigger a straight man. This was her attempt to emasculate him.

When people start talking to you like this and targeting you, as I've seen many times, it won't be long before they find a way to get you out of there. Shortly after these two arguments, I overheard a supervisor say, "He is almost out of here," referring to Mr. Rap-a-Lot. Within a month, we said goodbye to him. The members of the Wolfpack had done it again. Mr Rap-a-Lot argued that it was hypocritical for 34X34 to complain about him sleeping when she could be found in the break area for hours herself. I know for a fact that she sleeps more than he does, and on top of that, she has more responsibility as the lead of the entire platform. Her pay rank is level five or six, while Mr. Rap-a-Lot, no longer driving, has dropped to level four. If you break it down, the person who is sleeping the most and costing the most money due to their lack of productivity is 34X34, and everyone, including supervisors, knows that. But it's acceptable if you're part of the Wolfpack.

CHAPTER 17

Attacks from All Angles

Mr Slick has made Gothic and me the center of attention on the platform. As mature workers, we don't need supervision to fulfill our responsibilities, unlike most of our coworkers who require constant direction. Supervisors and expediters from Tours Two and Three consistently praise us as their great workers, noting how operations suffer when we're absent.

Our work ethic stands in stark contrast to others, particularly our team lead, who regularly vanishes, and Carmen Sandiego, nicknamed after the popular show because management constantly searches for him. Gothic revealed he deliberately makes himself scarce to avoid responsibility. Then there's Turtle, who moves at a glacial pace, pretending to be busy while accomplishing nothing. Ironically, management overlooks these behaviors but scrutinizes Gothic and me relentlessly.

When we arrive at 10:00 PM, truck drivers are already waiting. Lips invariably appear, barking orders to assert her authority, particularly ironic given her compromised position after being caught with Bob, one of the drivers, in his truck. She compensates by belittling others and bragging about her six-figure salary.

To avoid the hostile atmosphere, we took breaks near the recycling area, a spot Mr. Slick had shown me where old-timers gathered. His behavior grew increasingly strange, once bringing his heated lunch outside in freezing weather, claiming he'd forgotten utensils in his car, despite his usual break area being closer to the parking lot.

The harassment escalated when we chose a spot to sit during breaks. Our area was repeatedly blocked, forcing us to clear obstacles daily. The situation peaked when someone cordoned off our space with caution tape, making it look like a crime scene. While Section A workers had pallets and Section C enjoyed proper chairs, we were denied any seating.

Section B, our area, demands the most physical effort, constant lifting, pulling, pushing, and now mail scanning. During peak season, despite being the platform's central hub for mail processing, we're chronically understaffed. Tour 3 starts with eight workers, but once they leave, our Mail Handler Assistants (MHAs) get reassigned to the line operation, which needs only two or three people but maintains seven or eight workers.

Meanwhile, 34X34, our platform lead, spends hours sleeping at the "bus stop" break area with several MHAs. When I approached Supervisor Naij about this imbalance, she deflected, claiming she couldn't override 34X34's decisions. To prove my point, I challenged her to check the bus stop or ask about basic operational details, questions that would go unanswered since 34X34 hadn't been on the platform for hours.

The harassment extends beyond seating arrangements. Equipment drivers intentionally block our path, delaying mail movement just to socialize. It's disturbing to watch people who've never had negative interactions with us join in the harassment simply to align themselves with the Wolfpack and Hyena clique.

Most frustrating is how quickly they spread distorted versions of any interaction. If they had told the truth, it would have been clear that Gothic and I never instigated conflicts; we merely responded to provocations. They create confrontations to gain social currency, treating workplace harassment like a popularity contest.

Security cameras and unbiased witnesses would confirm that we're consistently on the defensive, reacting to orchestrated provocations rather than starting problems.

CHAPTER 18

My First Fight with 34X34

At this point, I'm feeling incredibly frustrated. People are deliberately making my work life miserable. Despite my documented chronic back issue known to management, no one provides the help we need in the swamped B section. It's disheartening to see MHAs (Mail Handler Assistants) sleeping by the bus stop while I work hard. Supervisors continue to ignore our staffing issues despite my complaints.

This frustration leads me to reflect on my choices. My Fitbit records about 17,000 steps during each eight-hour shift. When I voice my concerns to my supervisor, hoping for change, she merely relays them to 34X34, who responds, "I don't give a fuck; he's always bitching." The most infuriating remark was, "Fuck him, he's always complaining. He'll be all right."

I respond, "Learn how to do your job because you're failing as a leader." That's when 34X34 erupts, reminiscent of the incident with Mr. Rap-a-Lot. "Stop complaining, be a man, stop being a gay faggot," she yells, even commenting on my pants. Despite her being lesbian, I never disrespect her with homophobic slurs. Yet, she projects her issues onto me.

My complaint to management and the union yields nothing, no follow-up, no discipline. 34X34 continues, making work difficult for Gothic and me. As part of the Wolfpack, she's protected. Supervisor Naij does the bare minimum, spending hours on personal calls or eating. Later, I discover she's also part of the Wolfpack, explaining her inaction.

I'm forced to hand-jack full trucks of Gaylords (large cardboard containers) despite available equipment drivers. A task that takes a double fork driver seven minutes requires 25 minutes of manual labor from us. Management's response? "That's your job. You're a mail handler." This isn't about the job description; and it's about the efficient use of resources.

34X34 turns equipment drivers against us, saying, "They told me to tell you to unload door 20; I don't know why when they have hand jacks over there." The drivers now tell us, "You all have hand jacks; you should use them." Hand jacking heavy BMCs (Bulk Mail Containers) and APCs (Automated Parcel Containers) becomes management's way of punishing those who choose not to drive equipment.

I stopped driving months ago after being overworked, manipulated by Mr. Slick, and dealing with post-dental surgery medication that prohibited operating machinery. When 34X34 demands I drive equipment despite my medicated state, I refuse. This leads to a confrontation with Miss Butterfly, a supervisor more concerned with popularity than respect.

Miss Butterfly sent me home without investigation simply because 34X34 ordered it. The union representative assured me this was improper and promised compensation, which I still haven't received. Multiple incidents remain unresolved: missing pay, ignored grievances and concealed altercations.

34X34's violent confrontation with Pat exemplifies the systemic issues. She provokes him with homophobic slurs and cruel comments about his newborn. After losing the fight, she returns with brass knuckles. Yet no official report exists, another example of the system protecting her.

She rarely confronts other women, knowing she can't play the victim if beaten by one. This isn't her first or second incident with workers. I've documented everything, warning plant manager about her liability. If she injures someone, my paper trail will prove management knew the risks.

This toxic environment, where accountability disappears, and abuse thrives, cannot continue. While 34X34 maintains her position through fear and connections, workers face increasing hostility for doing their jobs efficiently. The documentation exists for anyone willing to investigate, but they'll need to protect witnesses' anonymity to get the truth.

CHAPTER 19

Shit Hit the Fan

The usual gossip and attacks have intensified, with the Wolfpack deliberately making our jobs harder. Every time we visit the recycling area, we hear the exit door to the loading docks open, even though it's distant from the main recycling door. I often hear movement, but whenever I investigate, the sounds cease.

One day, while Gothic and I were at the recycling area, me smoking and her vaping, I heard the door open, followed by distinct high-heeled footsteps. Then came Lips' voice. At 6'3", I spotted her before she noticed me. She was on the phone, scanning the area intently. Upon finding what, or who, she sought, she fell silent, turning her full attention to us.

"What are you guys doing here?" she asked.

"We're taking our 15-minute break," I replied.

"You can't be back here; it's not a designated smoking area," she retorted, adding more that I don't recall, my ADHD blurring her words. MDO Lips then escorted us out.

The next day, while Gothic and I sat on stacked pallets, Lips passed by with an odd look. Shortly after, Gothic was called to the general clerk's office. We exchanged surprised glances, and I felt uneasy, remembering Lips' earlier expression.

When Gothic returned, she looked dejected and began packing without a word. Before I could ask, she said, "Lips moved me to the line."

"Why?" I asked.

"She said you and I sitting on the pallet looked inappropriate and made some coworkers uncomfortable." Gothic gathered her belongings and left. Deeply upset by their treatment of good employees, Gothic and I discussed our next move by phone. Later, seeing Lips surrounded by workers near the priority mail area, staring and talking as I passed, I approached her.

"MDO Lips, I'd like to talk to you," I said.

"About what?" she asked.

"I don't understand why Gothic was moved," I explained. "This impacts the platform because no one else works as efficiently as she does, and the line operation isn't part of the platform. Since she's not an MHA, union rules prohibit this move." Surrounded by her entourage, Lips responded condescendingly, prompting me to criticize management's emotional rather than logical decision-making.

Lips scheduled a meeting for 6:30 AM. I agreed, reiterating my confusion about why sitting on a pallet was deemed inappropriate. Returning to the platform, I found Pastor and Miss Outspoken, a candid trainee, in the B section. They asked about the commotion, incredulous when I explained Gothic's removal. When I asked if Gothic and I sitting together made them uncomfortable, they responded, "Hell no, how could it?"

The pastor noted Lips' habit of hugging drivers and sitting with them on pallets. Miss Outspoken added, "I don't know why that bitch is messing with you guys. All I see you two do is work hard. Who does she think she is, saying you sitting together is inappropriate after being caught in a truck?"

She continued, "The president (a well-liked coworker) and I saw Lips at a hotel with married Bob, the same guy from the truck incident. After his wife came here wanting to confront Lips about fucking her husband, Lips' car was later found vandalized. I think Bob's wife did it. But despite all that, Lips still meets Bob at hotels. I guess that's better than the USPS Plantation trucks."

Miss Outspoken hadn't noticed Lips passing by. Lips, clearly embarrassed from overhearing the conversation, quickly left the area.

CHAPTER 20

I Refuse to Be Intimidated or Silenced

It's nearly 6:30 AM when I knock on the general clerk's office door, waiting to be let in for my meeting with MDO Lips. A young lady opens the door and asks, "Who are you here to see?"

"I have a meeting with Lips scheduled for 6:30," I reply.

"Okay, give me a moment; let me call her," she says. After a brief conversation with Lips, the young lady instructs me to follow her to Lips' office. Upon entering, I see Lips sitting there alongside her supervisor, whom I've nicknamed Brother Man (who later became an MDO). I take a seat, and Lips has this attitude as if she's preparing to assert her authority. She wears the same look she adopts when she comes to the platform to belittle the other women that the drivers are actually hitting on.

"So, how can I help you?" she asks. I want to know the real reason Gothic was moved. Her explanation that Gothic and I sitting together looked inappropriate simply doesn't hold water; I haven't done anything wrong. I was just sitting down and talking to a coworker like everyone else does every night.

I begin to explain how much work Gothic, and I manage without any help each night and how people seem to disappear while we're working, but nobody addresses that issue. As I continue, Lips tries to downplay my workload. I almost forgot to mention that Lips once told me, "For your age, how do you get the energy to run circles around these younger workers?" She's always complimented my work ethic, but today, she feels the need to undermine my claims about people disappearing. Why do they call on those individuals every night, five to ten times? When I say "disappearing," I mean people are gone for hours. The lead is absent for hours. We're essentially doing the work of six people, and now the one person who worked efficiently with me is gone. How can you expect the platform to run smoothly when management isn't doing its job? They're only making things worse.

By the time I finish speaking, Lips retorts, "I know you're going to tell me how much you work and how people disappear." The reason she knows that is that it's true; I've complained about disappearing workers to various supervisors countless times, but nothing has been done. Lips then moves to the side of the table, pulls out freshly printed sheets of my time punches, and starts reading, "On this date, you took a five-minute break; on this date, you took a break at this time; on this date, you went on..." She continues listing the dates of my five-minute breaks. But when I'm the one doing all the work, how can I only take a 15-minute break while my coworkers are gone for hours? That's exactly what I told her. "Why do you think that when you come to the platform, everything is done, no matter how hectic it gets? It's because someone is doing the work while all these people are disappearing."

However, she spreads those documents across the table and asks, "Do you still want to have this conversation?" I expected Brother Man to stand up and say, "Stop trying to bully him", or that it's not right to intimidate me. But he just sat there in silence. I remember hearing people refer to him as Lips' flunky or bodyguard because he always agrees with whatever Lips says. After all, she is the queen of the Wolfpack. I am shocked and completely at a loss for words. If this isn't intimidation, I don't know what is.

I replied, "Yes, I still want to have this conversation, but I feel your approach is wrong. I came to ask about what happened to my coworker and how it would impact the platform, yet you've taken the time to print out all my timestamps just to intimidate me. That's not right."

"Do you want me to discuss this timestamp issue with your supervisor?" she asked.

"Sure, you can if you want to," I replied. After the conversation, I left the office, determined not to let her tactics intimidate me. This is wrong, and workers should not have to endure this.

CHAPTER 21

Another Useless Platform Meeting

"Attention all platform workers: Please report to Section A for a platform meeting." Here we go again with yet another useless meeting. It's pointless because they discuss the same issues every time without implementing any real solutions. The topic is usually about equipment drivers disappearing and other workers vanishing when it's time to load and offload trucks. Management knows who they should talk to privately because the same individuals are consistently mentioned by those of us who actually work. However, management prefers to be friendly with those who don't contribute and those who vanish, making it difficult for them to address these individuals directly in their offices. The easiest solution for them is to hold a general meeting, which only prevents people from working and ultimately leads to backlogs.

During these meetings, I'm constantly checking the time and glancing at Section B because we have specific trucks that need to leave at certain times. Somehow, since we're left to fend for ourselves, we're forced to do the work of six people. To make matters worse, they schedule meetings during peak dispatch times. This is why I despise these meetings; they fail to address the real issues and only generalize the problems. Those who need private conversations about their performance never receive them. This cycle of useless platform meetings will continue every other week.

Now, I have to listen to the Queen of Disappearances, 34X34, open her mouth and say things like, "We all need to work harder. We're paid to work eight hours a day, and I don't understand why we're not doing that." Some people roll their eyes, thinking, "Girl, shut the hell up! You barely work for two hours a night, and half the time, you're somewhere knocked out, high as a kite." Everyone knows that 34X34 sleeps at the bus stop, and those who work with her constantly complain about it. Nothing has been done, and nothing will be done until someone speaks out about her behavior because she is protected by someone in management. From all I've experienced and witnessed, they cover for her every action.

But back to the meeting. This time, Lips attended and began addressing the group. She wanted to remind everyone to be mindful of their behavior in front of the cameras, claiming they caught some people being inappropriate. I looked around, wondering who on earth she was referring to. As she spoke, I noticed she kept glancing at Gothic and me. After the meeting, she approached Gothic, who instructed her to go to the line. It felt like all the attention shifted to Gothic, and she started walking away toward the line operations. I noticed a lot of whispering. Suddenly, the rumor spread through the building that Lips had caught Gothic and me being inappropriate on camera.

The ridiculous part was that Gothic's move led people to assume we were the ones Lips had caught on camera. I began noticing how many individuals were coming from various operations just to watch us. Gothic complained about people randomly approaching the line area to look at Gothic. I saw various individuals coming from different operations, likely to see the so-called offenders caught on camera. When people started asking me if it was true. Union Rep Miss Flower approached Gothic and me, saying, "I heard you two were caught on camera having sex." I asked her who had told her that, and she replied that Lips claimed she had footage of us being inappropriate, and now it was spreading through the building like wildfire. This rumor about us being caught on camera was causing quite a stir.

CHAPTER 22

It's Time to Sit Down with Miss Flower

With everything happening, the camera rumors, Gothic's unauthorized transfer, and our excessive workload, a meeting with Miss Flower was long overdue. Her office provided a sanctuary where we finally felt supported. She possessed the fighting spirit we needed for our battle against Lips, sharing what she knew about the alleged inappropriate behavior caught on camera. She encouraged us to file EEO complaints, which we readily agreed to. When Mr. Slick's name emerged in our conversation, her reaction spoke volumes. As a union rep, her demeanor suggested she knew more about his questionable conduct than she could reveal.

Mr. Slick's reputation for causing drama preceded him, but my immediate concern was clearing my name. I asked Miss Flower to demand the supposed video footage from Lips, confident that none existed since Gothic and I had never acted inappropriately. We knew Lips was fabricating the entire story.

Regarding Gothic's transfer to the line operation, Miss Flower immediately confirmed it violated protocol since Gothic was assigned to the platform. She committed to pursuing Gothic's reinstatement to the B section. Our discussion then shifted to addressing the broader issue of management's abuse and potential solutions.

I mentioned the town hall meetings that traditionally allowed employees to voice concerns to higher management. Miss Flower explained that despite repeated requests, no such meeting had been held in over five years. Management seemed reluctant to face the mounting grievances about their abusive practices.

In response, I proposed creating a digital town hall meeting. We could compile employee complaints, create a YouTube video, and share it with management. This digital platform would document our concerns and extend our reach beyond the facility. I just needed Miss Flower to help create a poster inviting employees to share their experiences.

The plan was to produce an impactful audio file enhanced with background music to convey our message effectively. Miss Flower enthusiastically embraced the idea, sending me a powerful flyer the next day:

"ENOUGH is ENOUGH!!!

WE (the employees) at the Incoming Mail Facility, a.k.a. the USPS Plantation (Linthicum, MD), stand collectively and say ENOUGH is ENOUGH! We have the RIGHT to come to work every day without FEAR, FEAR of slander, favoritism, disparate treatment, intimidation, humiliation, bullying, harassment, or any other inappropriate behavior. WE (the employees) will no longer allow abusive managers to mentally, physically, emotionally, and spiritually abuse us. We asked for a town hall meeting, and it was IGNORED. Now, the world will know our secrets. This is OUR town hall meeting. Now, you can finally HEAR our cries.

Postal MANAGEMENT has FAILED to adequately listen to us and address our hostile work environment. WE are here to say that YOU...MANAGEMENT must STOP the ABUSE. Since you won't listen to us, WE (the employees) can address and share our concerns here. Let's HEAL and FIGHT for our DIGNITY together. Contact ftn1211@yahoo.com and tell us about your ME-TOO toxic work environment experience."

CHAPTER 23

They Set Miss Outspoken Up

The Wolfpack's calculated setup of Miss Outspoken revealed their ruthless nature. During our supervisor Naij's absence, Lips seized the opportunity to assert her authority, relocating Gothic and summoning me to her office for intimidation. Upon Naij's return, something felt distinctly wrong. Typically, Naij treated Miss Outspoken with cautious respect, knowing her reputation for sharp responses and fearless confrontation. Even when addressing serious matters, Naij maintained a playful tone, carefully choosing her words to avoid Miss Outspoken's legendary verbal backlash.

Today was different. Naij deliberately confronted Miss Outspoken, seemingly provoking a reaction. Despite Miss Outspoken's warnings to back off, Naij persisted. The orchestrated nature of the encounter became clear when, at the height of the confrontation, Lips appeared. Rather than mediating, she escalated the situation, driving Miss Outspoken to an explosive outburst. I watched helplessly as police arrived to escort Miss Outspoken from the property, noting Lips' satisfied smirk.

Days later, I approached Supervisor Naij about the incident. I explained how Lips had manipulated the situation, using Naij as an unwitting pawn in her revenge plot. The catalyst? Miss Outspoken had earlier discussed Lips' affair with Bob, the truck driver, claiming to have evidence of their hotel rendezvous. Lips, desperate to suppress this information, orchestrated Miss Outspoken's removal without revealing her true motives. Naij's shock at this revelation confirmed her role as an unknowing participant in Lips' scheme.

The injustice of it all ignited a fire within me. Miss Outspoken, a single mother and dedicated eight-year employee, lost her livelihood because of a personal vendetta. The union's ineffectiveness in protecting employees like her underscores the urgent need for change. This incident, among countless others, compelled me to write this book. Every meaningful change begins with someone standing up and saying, "Enough." While I'm willing to work hard, I refuse to accept abuse as a condition of earning a living.

Writing this brings forth powerful emotions, but these feelings fuel my determination to share this story and inspire others to speak up against workplace injustice.

CHAPTER 24

Filing EEO. No, Miss Flower.

Gothic and I met with Miss Flower to discuss two pressing issues: the alleged inappropriate behavior footage and Gothic's transfer situation. Miss Flower reported that Lips kept evading her requests to see the video, claiming she was either busy or in meetings. The story then changed. Lips claimed it wasn't a video but rather a picture sent from headquarters. "I told you Lips was lying," I said to Miss Flower, urging her to demand any evidence Lips claimed to have, knowing no inappropriate behavior had occurred.

Regarding Gothic's transfer, Miss Flower explained that since the line operation wasn't part of the platform, Gothic simply needed to inform her supervisor about returning to her original position. It seemed straightforward enough. However, when Gothic approached Supervisor Naij with this request, she encountered unexpected resistance. Naij insisted she needed Lips' approval first. When Gothic attempted to contact Lips directly, she was told Lips was too busy to address the matter.

A week passed without any resolution. During our follow-up meeting with Miss Flower, we learned that Lips' story had completely unraveled. The alleged video had become a photograph, and finally, Lips admitted to Miss Flower that she had fabricated the entire situation. While Miss Flower seemed shocked by this revelation, Gothic and I weren't surprised; we had known all along that no evidence existed because nothing inappropriate had occurred.

Miss Flower then outlined the EEO complaint process and requested our statements. I asked her to document Lips' admission of lying about the evidence, believing this would finally hold Lips accountable for her actions against employees who simply wanted to earn a living and support their families. With a union representative's statement confirming Lips' deception, I thought we had an airtight case. I would soon learn otherwise.

Miss Flower concluded by addressing the ongoing confusion about Gothic's position, noting that Lips and Supervisor Naij seemed to be giving conflicting accounts. She promised to get us a definitive answer soon.

CHAPTER 25

The Roles Are Now Reversed

As word of my impending EEO complaint spread, I noticed increased activity among the Wolfpack members; lips, Ellen, Mr. Slick, and Supervisor Naij began holding frequent meetings. Their focus had shifted from their usual dynamics to orchestrating a defense against Gothic and me, particularly targeting my position in the B section.

Miss Flower's latest update revealed an unexpected twist: Gothic's transfer allegedly resulted from paperwork Mr. Slick had filed against her. Miss Flower's skeptical tone suggested she found this explanation dubious. The story had conveniently evolved from Lips' initial claim about inappropriate behavior caught on camera to this mysterious paperwork, documentation we'd never seen nor could anyone prove existed. More suspiciously, the line operation was suddenly being classified as part of the platform.

This new classification contradicted everything we knew. The union president and line workers all confirmed that historically, the line had never been considered part of the platform. Yet somehow, to justify keeping Gothic away from her assigned position and maintain our excessive workload, management had arbitrarily redefined these operational boundaries. Before departing the union office, I requested Miss Flower's statement for my EEO complaint. She assured me she'd provide it the following day.

Discussing these developments with Gothic, we recognized Mr. Slick's calculated strategy. He was poisoning opinions against Gothic before she could defend herself, orchestrating a preemptive character assassination. His goal was clear: paint her as unstable so any future statements she made would be automatically discredited. This manipulative damage control tactic revealed the extent of their determination to silence us.

CHAPTER 26

The Wolfpack Retaliates

Due to Gothic and my ongoing EEO case, Lips and her Wolfpack have begun to target us. Picture this: you're assigned to a line that previously had six to eight MHAs working, but now, everyone has been moved away, leaving you to manage alone. This is precisely what happened to Gothic. They removed all her support, forcing her to work the line by herself without any assistance. Even when others who were supposed to be present showed up, they either vanished or were redirected by management to other tasks, rather than helping Gothic.

Imagine the frustration of working hard, only to know that someone is intentionally trying to complicate your job. Gothic went from having ample support to being the sole person responsible for the workload of several. Meanwhile, management observed this situation, appearing to find it acceptable. It escalated to the point where Gothic had to search the entire property for equipment that the drivers were supposed to deliver. Instead of providing her with the necessary drivers, they made her walk around for two to three hours, looking for equipment to manage the mail, which delayed the entire process. She was left rushing and stressed because an MDO was neglecting her duties, choosing instead to create chaos in Gothic's work life, seemingly deriving enjoyment from it.

While I was virtually alone on the platform, people in the A and C sections merely stood by, watching me work without offering assistance. Instead, they giggled and laughed, relishing the sight of me laboring solo. What they didn't realize was that their inaction was causing mail delays. I was just one person, and my Fitbit was going crazy with the number of steps I took each night. I became so active that I started consuming protein shakes to keep up with the physical demands, as I was losing weight due to the excessive activity.

The situation worsened as I found myself being written up for every minor infraction. I frequently visited the General Clerk's office or the platform supervisor's office for reprimands. Within a month, I was called in regarding my attendance, to the point where a union representative remarked, "This isn't normal. How can they target you this many times when others have far worse attendance?" It became clear that they were attempting to frustrate me into calling off work, so they could keep writing me up and ultimately work towards suspending me.

I started documenting everything and sought Miss Flower's statement regarding the upcoming EEO case. However, something felt off, and I was determined to piece it all together.

CHAPTER 27

Miss Flower Is Acting Funny

Miss Flower's behavior had shifted noticeably. She stopped checking on us, and my requests for the EEO statement were met with constant delays. "Give me until Tuesday" became "tomorrow," and this cycle repeated for a month. Her usual passionate demeanor had dimmed, replaced by uncharacteristic low energy, especially during our discussions about workplace issues.

To understand this change, I arranged a meeting with her and Gothic. During our conversation, I carefully brought up specific topics to gauge her position. When discussing our EEO case, her disappointment was evident - the fighting spirit she once showed had vanished. Having witnessed her previous experiences with management's bullying, particularly from Lips, I understood her vulnerability. She, too, had been a target of their abuse.

My instincts suggested she was under pressure to withdraw from our case. When I asked her directly, her response confirmed these suspicions. After her apology, I knew we needed to find another path forward. This led me to seek help from the union president, whom I privately called Mr. Sweaty Eyes. He was a very large man, similar in build to the rapper Big Pun, and earned his nickname from his constantly watery eyes. His presence was further marked by an unfortunate lack of personal hygiene that followed him everywhere.

Despite these characteristics, meeting with him had become crucial for Gothic and me. I asked Miss Flower to set up the appointment.

CHAPTER 28

Our Meeting with Mr. Sweaty Eyes

We gathered, waiting for Mr. Sweaty Eyes to arrive for our meeting. When he finally walked in, he opened the door and stepped inside, leaving a lingering, unpleasant odor behind him. We followed, trying to hold our breath to avoid feeling nauseous. It was clear from my earlier remarks that he wasn't my favorite person on the property; I felt he wasn't doing his job properly.

Our first real interaction had been uncomfortable. As I walked by him one day, he called out, "Come here." I initially thought he was speaking to someone else and was surprised he felt he could talk to me that way. Sensing my discomfort, he quickly changed his approach and asked for my name instead.

Now, in his office, I began explaining what was happening and how people were treating me. It seemed like he had an excuse for every problem I brought up. Soon after we started talking, Miss Flower entered the room. I continued to share my feelings and mentioned my upcoming EEO case, stressing that I needed support from the union. However, his responses made me feel like he wasn't truly on my side.

When I told him what Lips had done, Miss Flower confirmed my account, yet he didn't express any concern for our situation. Instead, he asked, "What do you want to do, get Lips fired?" and spoke about how long Lips had been there as if that mattered more than our experiences. His tone and behavior felt dismissive, making me think he was more aligned with management than with me.

After our conversation, it felt like Miss Flower distanced herself from our case. To sum it up, she didn't show up for the EEO hearing, nor did she provide any statement. The president also remained silent, never asking how the case went or offering to support me. He didn't mention the critical things Miss Flower had said in the office, claiming that Lips told her he had caught us on camera being inappropriate, only to later say that Lips claimed it was all a lie.

Without the union's help and unable to reach anyone that day, I had to rely on a coworker to represent me during the EEO proceedings. I have to be honest; the way the EEO agency handled my case made me feel like their system was designed to filter out claims that weren't strong enough to sue USPS. From my experience and that of others, it seemed they didn't genuinely care about helping people with EEO cases.

Ultimately, my case was dismissed. That same night, right after the hearing, Lips had them call me to the General Clerk's office to issue yet another write-up for attendance. If anyone thinks this isn't retaliation, I don't know what else to call it. It felt like a clear message from her, showcasing her power: she was untouchable.

CHAPTER 29

I Cannot Let Them Get Away with This. It's Time to Fight Back.

Now that I feel like my back is against the wall, I decided that we are on our own. No one in that property is able to assist us in any way possible to get the resolution that we want. I believe if you make enough noise, somebody will hear you, and this book is a part of that noise. I decided to use the concept that I shared with Miss Flower to make my next move. I had Gothic record a voice audio about all the things she has been through on that property, especially all the run-ins with Lips. I also made an audio recording of my experiences and run-ins with Lips and management, and I think I said something else about the union, too, because they are useless. After I got the audio, I put it together with a little bit of music in the background and posted it on YouTube, but I posted it as restricted so only those who actually have the link could view the video. I began to send a lot of emails out to different people, attaching the audio of the things we are going through at the USPS Plantation. Plus, I did a lot of praying for guidance.

CHAPTER 30

God Is Good!

After a challenging year dealing with Lips, the Wolfpack, and Mr. Slick, today felt different from the moment it began. Pulling into work, I scored the best parking spot in the lot when another car coincidentally pulled away. Then, as I stepped out, my phone slipped from my pocket. In a moment of unexpected agility, I managed a quick soccer-style kick that sent it flying back into my hand - not a scratch on the screen!

The day's good fortune continued when a coworker casually mentioned Lips would be leaving in two weeks. Initially skeptical, I heard the same news from several other sources, making it harder to dismiss. Could we finally be catching a break?

I immediately called Gothic, which was still assigned to the "newly designated" platform line. "Guess what?" I could barely contain my excitement as I shared the news about Lips' potential departure. The possibility alone lifted our spirits.

Later, I spotted MDO Lips during her rounds. Her presence had changed noticeably - gone was her commanding stride in those wedge heels, replaced by uncertain steps that seemed to mirror her diminishing authority. Her typically confident demeanor had faded, and she appeared subdued. Then came the confirmation: I overheard her personally telling someone about her upcoming departure in two weeks. My face lit up with joy, though I maintained my professional composure despite wanting to celebrate openly.

That weekend, Gothic and I went out to celebrate this welcome development. After everything we'd endured, the news of Lips' departure felt like freedom. Finally, a positive change was coming to our workplace. Good riddance!

CHAPTER 31

BYE-BYE BITCH! I Mean Lips

The truth about Lips' departure emerged gradually. Contrary to initial appearances, she hadn't left voluntarily. According to circulating rumors, management had presented her with an ultimatum: transfer to a facility in the Carolinas or face termination from USPS. She chose the transfer, leaving behind a complex legacy among her colleagues.

A domino effect followed her exit. Mr Slick was next - rumors of his retirement or reassignment proved true when he transferred to another location. Then, Supervisor Naij departed, choosing an entirely different career path. Miss Flower's disappearance was more mysterious - after the EEO case, she simply vanished, and I haven't seen her at work for nearly a year.

Gothic has returned to the B section, restoring our working partnership and bringing back a sense of normalcy I'd missed. While it might seem like the perfect conclusion - with all the troublesome figures gone - this isn't the end of our story. The workplace has transformed, but new challenges continue to emerge, reminding us that change is constant and our journey continues.

CHAPTER 32

Guess Who's Back?

One day, while unloading a truck, that unmistakable sensation of being watched crept over me. You know that feeling - when instinct makes you turn around, and your eyes lock with someone staring at you? That's exactly what happened when I spotted Lips glaring at me from the platform. The air suddenly felt suffocating. What was this nightmare doing back at USPS Plantation? How had this aggressive, stomping menace managed to return?

Her displeasure was evident, especially when she noticed Gothic working on the platform. She quickly summoned the supervisors to the A section for a meeting, but something was different. This wasn't the commanding presence she once projected. The supervisors spoke to her with unexpected confidence, clearly showing they no longer feared her authority. She noticed this shift, too, and after a few failed attempts to reassert her dominance, she disappeared back to wherever she came from. That was the last we saw of Lips.

CHAPTER 33

A Farewell Prayer for Lips

Dear Lord,

I bring MDO Lips before you with a burdened heart. I pray for her longevity, not from spite, but hoping she'll comprehend how her actions have affected others. May she receive what she has given, both positive and negative, and find healing through these experiences.

I understand that those who inflict pain often carry their own wounds. Guide her toward redemption and the wisdom to seek forgiveness. You know the countless workdays she transformed into hardships and the many hearts she wounded. Please bring peace to those she has hurt.

Lord, I struggle to find genuine compassion for her while still processing my own healing. Though forgiveness remains my goal, these feelings weigh heavily upon me. Grant me the strength to speak my truth.

Lips, I don't wish you harm. Instead, I hope you experience the same treatment you showed others. May your best efforts be met with the same scrutiny you gave ours, and may your mistakes be noticed more than your achievements.

May life teach you the lessons needed for growth and transformation. And as you walk this path, may the Lord grant you the forgiveness that I am still learning to give.

Amen.

CHAPTER 34

A Time for Reflection

When I started at USPS Plantation, I brought enthusiasm and a genuine desire to help others, and I was determined to excel in every task. The harsh treatment I received stood in stark contrast to the positivity I offered. I wasn't there just to collect a paycheck - I came to earn my place and exceed expectations in the B Section platform, always ready to help anyone in need without being asked.

My colleagues would tell you about the numerous times I supported them through difficulties. Yet this kindness often made me a target, with some choosing loyalty to friends over acknowledging my goodwill. Even as people sought my help during unfair treatment, knowing I would advocate for them, I gradually changed. I withdrew, stopped helping, and let anger and resentment take over. Depression crept in, and I barely recognized myself anymore.

Like a white shirt worn without care, I felt stained by resentment toward management and peer unkindness. My willingness to help was questioned as if compassion were a weakness. This journey revealed itself to be bigger than me - many share these burdens but stay silent, fearing consequences.

I realized how easily I could have become another tragic headline - someone broken by workplace isolation and mistreatment. Instead of channeling my energy destructively, I chose to rise above those who tried to diminish me.

This reflection serves as a call for unity. While someone told me, "You can never change Postal," I believe we can inspire collective change. As USPS workers, we have the power to create a workplace focused solely on our duties, free from harassment and intimidation. Together, we can transform our environment into one of mutual support rather than fear.

CHAPTER 35

Oh No, Not Again!

Just when I thought the chaos had ended, Mr. Slick began making unexpected appearances at USPS Plantation. He'd stand in the A section with the platform supervisor, silently watching Gothic and me work. Then "2 Face" approached me with news of Mr. Slick's supposed retirement plans, claiming he'd heard it directly from him.

2 Face explained that Mr. Slick had suddenly acted friendly toward him, suggesting he felt displaced at his new workplace. This behavior was typical of 2 Face - he thrived on gossip, drawing people in with the latest news, only to speak negatively about them later. He'd shared stories about the pastor, Lips, Bob, and Mr. Slick, yet maintained a facade of friendship with each of them.

I've learned to be strategic with information at work. I maintain mental notes of everyone's connections and behaviors, using this knowledge carefully. When necessary, I share specific details with certain union reps, knowing they'll spread the information to intended targets. While they believe they're circulating rumors, they're actually delivering exactly what I want to be heard.

As I develop this book, I deliberately share excerpts and videos with select union reps, anticipating the information will reach management. This strategy helps ease the workplace pressure they've been applying. The moment I release certain details, I notice shifts in management's behavior.

When 2 Face mentioned Mr. Slick's retirement, I expressed doubt, explaining his continued presence at our facility. "He spends time here just watching Gothic work," I told him. "Mark my words - he'll return to USPS Plantation. His obsession with Gothic makes it inevitable."

"You really think he's coming back?" 2 Face asked.

"I'm certain of it," I replied.

CHAPTER 36

Changes on the Platform

The platform's atmosphere has recently changed. In the A section, our new expediter Pastor leads what appears to be a perfect life - a happy marriage, flourishing children, and regular family vacations abroad. She often shares these stories, oblivious that her audience consists mainly of single, dissatisfied women. Several MHAs also work in this section.

B section includes me, Gothic, and Slow Mo (nicknamed Turtle) - an older worker who's perfected the illusion of productivity while doing very little. Carmen San Diego frequently vanishes during shifts, prompting multiple searches nightly. Batman, sporting braces that don't stop his constant chatter, started as a dedicated worker but transformed into another phone-focused employee who corners people with endless sports talk.

My "aunt," a church-going elderly woman with a troubled history involving crack, earned her nickname from Gothic because we share a birth month. Her unpredictable mood swings continue - she'll leave for her car briefly, return singing, then suddenly shift to anger. These erratic behaviors suggest her struggles aren't entirely in the past.

The B Section rotates between several expediters: Ninja Turtle primarily, with Light Skin and Dust Cuz filling in during her absences. Light Skin stands out as the most pleasant to work with, maintaining a consistently professional approach. In the C Section, Miss Peace excels as our best expediter. Though I've never seen her face behind her mask, her beautiful nail art and, more importantly, her unwavering kindness make her remarkable. She treats everyone with the same respect, regardless of workplace drama.

While the rest of C Section's staff doesn't warrant detailed mention, I must note our disappointment in Purple, our new supervisor, whose recent behavior falls significantly short of what we expected.

CHAPTER 37

Crossing Boundaries

Boundaries are crucial for maintaining a respectful and balanced life. They clearly define what we are comfortable with and what we are not. Without them, we risk experiencing a lack of respect from others who fail to recognize our limits. By establishing boundaries, we communicate the importance of our well-being, fostering healthier relationships and a more peaceful existence.

I reached a breaking point where I realized I had endured enough chaos around me. I decided that if anyone challenges me, I will respond even more assertively. Observing others, I notice many are unaware that I exhibit some autistic traits, which means my way of processing things is unique. I can quickly identify flaws and errors when necessary, and I realized it was time to organize my thoughts and experiences.

I started analyzing every incident I encountered, reflecting on what I could do differently or how I could adjust my approach. Each night at work, I replay the day's events in my mind, looking for areas of improvement. I've identified several faults in various situations, and now, when people confront me, I counter with what they're not doing right. I'm confident that no one can physically intimidate me, and I'm not afraid of anyone. I also don't believe they are smarter than I am, so I've decided to approach the game differently.

CHAPTER 38

Why Are You All Not Holding People Accountable?

It's frustrating to watch my coworkers disappear for hours while no one holds them accountable. I have complained to management numerous times, yet nothing has changed. I've spoken to MDOs, and still, there are no improvements. I've raised concerns about 34X34 disappearing for hours; everyone knows she doesn't do anything all night, yet somehow management overlooks it. It's gotten to the point where I've started to question who 34X34 is related to. Every time I ask about her connections, people burst into laughter, often to the point where I consider becoming a comedian. My first set would start with, "Who is 34X34 related to?" It's an automatic crowd-pleaser.

I've also inquired about Carmen San Diego and Slow Mo, a.k.a. Turtle, and how they are allowed to vanish for hours with no consequences. They are drivers being paid at Level 5, and when they disappear, Gothic and I are left to physically pull and push heavy mail across various operations. When I complain to supervisors and MDOs, I'm met with the excuse that they are on break. How many hours do they get to disappear?

Oh, my bad; I mean, go on break while Gothic and I are stuck working harder, only to receive Level 4 pay?

We are loading and unloading, scanning, consolidating, and sometimes even tagging late mail tasks that are supposed to be assigned to someone else. Yet Gothic and I are held responsible for tagging mail when the designated person is absent. Meanwhile, we have MHAs and other mail handlers who aren't doing anything at all. They even have us pulling items from operations that aren't ours.

The metro mail that is supposed to be moved to the platform by equipment drivers should be handled efficiently. In other tours, the metro mail is brought to the platform by equipment drivers, and all the unequipped drivers have to do is push it into the trucks. This process is efficient and keeps us from breaking our backs. But because management wants to complicate our jobs, it leads to inefficiencies and delays in mail delivery.

CHAPTER 39

Setting Boundaries for Batman

Batman's work ethic deteriorated quickly after his initial show of diligence. I first addressed this with him directly, then with Pastor, the expediter, who dismissed my concerns. When he became the B section's least productive worker, I began reporting to management, but only after attempting to resolve things personally.

One day, Supervisor Purple assigned Gothic and me to unload the Sephora truck after our break. We prepared by placing APCs inside beforehand. Upon returning, we found Batman and Slow Mo already working there. While organizing nearby, I went to retrieve some APCs for mail consolidation. Batman confronted me aggressively, claiming I hadn't contributed to the setup. When I explained Purple's instructions, he escalated, calling me names and accusing me of being a "snitch."

The situation intensified as he challenged me to meet at 6:30 outside. While others found entertainment in his display, they didn't understand my capability for self-defense. Throughout the shift, I calmly suggested meeting at the closed movie theater, framing it as "sparring" to avoid legal issues. I noticed him becoming evasive, likely seeking support from others.

What Batman didn't realize was my experience with physical confrontations. I've handled multiple opponents before and have documented strength records at arcade punching machines. Before our scheduled meeting, management called me to the clerk's office. MDO Brother Man wanted my account first, likely concerned I'd leave early for the confrontation.

I explained everything transparently, emphasizing that I wouldn't accept being disrespected or intimidated. My ability to analyze people revealed Batman's nature - all talk, used to intimidating others with loud behavior but unprepared when someone stands firm.

He ultimately sought management's intervention and transferred to a different tour. Now, he completely avoids eye contact and interaction. Though someone named Marblehead apparently encouraged his behavior, neither of them understood my readiness to defend myself if confronted.

CHAPTER 40

The Importance of Confidentiality

Management and union representatives often misuse confidential information, gossiping about the very people they should protect. I've experienced this firsthand, which led to Batman labeling me a "snitch" after supervisors revealed my complaints about inactive coworkers.

Trust forms the foundation of any healthy workplace relationship. When supervisors breach confidentiality, they create serious problems and destroy essential communication channels. For instance, when a supervisor tells someone, "Michael said you're not working," they spark needless conflicts. Similarly, if an employee reports concerning behavior requesting anonymity for safety, a manager who reveals "Tommy said this about you" endangers the reporter and discourages future incident reporting.

Without confidence in management's discretion, dangerous situations emerge. I witnessed this when Lips publicly threatened me over a shift dispute. Private union discussions becoming public gossip further erodes trust in both union representation and management, fostering an unsafe environment.

When workers can't safely voice concerns or seek solutions, frustration festers. Despite having management structures supposedly designed for worker support, the lack of genuine assistance breeds resentment and negativity toward the company. This often leads to acting out behaviors that wouldn't occur if employees felt heard and protected.

Confidentiality remains essential for workplace health. Like any organization, USPS functions best with strong trust and open communication. This only happens when management prioritizes confidentiality and handles employee concerns with appropriate discretion and respect.

CHAPTER 41

Miserable Ninja Turtle

The Ninja Turtle is a young woman who is just a few inches shy of being classified as a little person. Back in the day, people might have referred to her as a midget, but that term is now considered inappropriate. The politically correct term is "little person," as far as I know. I nicknamed her Ninja Turtle because, based on her body and facial features, if you were to put a shell on her back and give her one of those masks with eye holes, the kind the Ninja Turtles wear, she could easily double as a body double for any of the Ninja Turtle characters in a Hollywood movie.

Ninja Turtle came into the B section of the platform as a fill-in when we didn't have any expediter available. Initially, everything seemed fine when she took over in that role, but I soon realized that she wasn't very focused and didn't genuinely want to learn how to do her job properly. Instead of taking notes from Pastor, she preferred seeking attention from truck drivers or having friends come to the expediter desk to chit-chat and gossip.

I remember when Ninja Turtle first shaved her hair and started wearing it short. I could tell she felt uncomfortable since it was the first time many people had seen her with such a drastic change. Being someone who can read energy, I wanted to cheer her up and help her feel more confident as she walked around the building. I approached her and said, "You got a haircut! Oh, I like it!" She replied, "Really?" I said, "Yeah, it really fits you." She thanked me, saying, "Thank you so much. I was feeling a little weird about it." I reassured her, "No, you shouldn't! I love it. It looks good on you." She left that interaction feeling good about herself, which was my goal.

However, I soon began to notice some negative traits she had, particularly her tendency to bring others down with her words. I remember wearing a black button-up Docker brand work shirt. It's a common choice for work attire, and I was not the only one wearing it. One day, she saw me and jokingly said, "You came to work in your happy hour shirt." Considering that we were on good terms, I laughed at the joke. However, when she repeated the same comment later, it felt less like a friendly jab. Throughout the night, she continued to make the "happy hour shirt" joke, and I began to realize she wasn't saying it from a good place. What started as a playful exchange turned into something intended for others to laugh at.

She kept repeating the joke to different people, and it became clear that it was no longer just a joke; it was a way to mock me. You can't tell me it's okay to say the same thing to more than ten different people and laugh about it every time. I began to assess her behavior and realized that this young lady was miserable, as everything she said seemed aimed at bringing others down.

I recalled how she made fun of a very short truck driver who came in frequently. What struck me as odd was that before she started teasing him, she was always in his face, trying to get his attention. Every time he arrived, she was the first to talk to him, as if she genuinely wanted to connect. One day, when he was conversing with another platform worker, she burst in, trying to be the loudest person in the room, and even hugged him. But when she noticed he had a girlfriend, it seemed to upset her. She then asked him for a picture, and when he showed it to her, she went off on his girlfriend, laughing loudly and saying that the man's girlfriend looked like Pastor T.D. Jakes.

Suppose you're familiar with T.D. Jake and his viral quote, "Have you been swallowed? Have you been swallowed up?" you can imagine how she teased this man, saying his girl looked like T.D. Jakes and repeating "swallowed, swallowed up" to the point where I could see the embarrassment on his face. It was baffling how she could be so friendly with him daily until he revealed he had someone, and then she resorted to teasing him about his girlfriend.

I've mentioned before how the Pastor often boasts about her husband and their amazing kids, and it's wonderful to see your children doing well; you can't help but talk about them. However, I don't think Pastor truly knows how to read a room. If she did, she would realize that some people around her are struggling. How can you talk about how amazing your husband is for taking you and your kids on vacation when, if you look around, those you're telling don't even have pets, partners, or children? They are often lonely and miserable, so jealousy is likely to arise, especially when Ninja Turtle talks about the pastor.

What I mentioned previously about people often saying, "That's my girl" or "That's my boy," holds true, but Ninja Turtle always adds, "That's my girl, but..." before including something negative. Those comments don't sound like something someone who genuinely likes another person would say. Sometimes, I want to tell Pastor to strengthen her relationship and focus on her family instead of engaging with side distractions because she is blessed with an amazing husband and wonderful kids.

I once spoke to her privately and asked, "What's the issue with your husband? Why aren't you more into him?" When she mentioned it was because he's out of shape, I couldn't help but think that Pastor could afford to lose a few pounds as well. My suggestion would have been that if she and her husband worked out together, they would both look amazing.

But I think about the kind of people I've seen Pastor talk to. From the outside looking in, her husband appears very gentle, yet she seems to prefer a "ghetto" type of man. At one point, she was with a guy I called "Silver Face." He was younger and a bit hood, and it was clear he didn't have any respect for her. That's what I found so perplexing: why would you let other men disrespect you when you have a loving husband who cares about you? It made no sense. It seems she enjoys the rough treatment from the people she interacts with, while her husband is probably more educated, judging by some of the things she posts.

CHAPTER 42

Purple, I am so disappointed in you.

Purple, our platform supervisor known for her initially purple-dyed hair, had a misconception about Gothic and me due to influence from Platform Lead 34X34 and the Wolfpack. Her initial aggressive approach and micromanagement made work challenging, despite our proven competence.

While Purple spent time socializing with less productive workers, we remained focused on our tasks. Though she was considered a "cool" supervisor, it was discouraging to see hardworking employees overlooked while others received attention.

Through observation, Purple discovered we were the platform's most dedicated workers, contrary to her initial judgment. In a candid office conversation, she admitted, "At first, I thought you guys were the problem, but you don't bother anyone. You just work hard." She recognized that others, not us, were causing issues.

After taking one night off due to mental exhaustion, our absence highlighted our significance. Even MDO Brother Man had to fill in. Upon our return, Purple acknowledged, "I didn't realize how much work you do." Our efficiency and independence, developed over two years, had made our contribution seem effortless.

Gothic and I managed the B section with minimal support. When either of us was absent, it affected operations significantly. My aunt's decision to leave work upon learning of my absence demonstrated our impact.

As compliments about our work ethic reached Purple, including praise from truck drivers, her attitude transformed. She defended us, stating, "I don't know why they keep bothering both of you. All you two do is work." This recognition improved our attendance and motivation.

However, pressure mounted as others grew uncomfortable with our recognition. The focus shifted to trivial issues, like our seating area near a "Do Not Block" sign, while significant problems like facility maintenance, substance abuse, and mail delays were ignored.

I noticed patterns suggesting intentional mail delays to overwhelm Purple's shift. A midnight delivery during peak season revealed Miss Beef Patty's involvement in holding mail, though Purple remained unaware of the manipulation.

Despite mounting pressure and criticism about her support of us, Purple stayed loyal. She began informing us of her days off, concerned for our wellbeing in her absence. The situation exposed a complex dynamic where Purple's support made her a target, caught between defending efficientworkers and yielding to external pressures.

CHAPTER 43

Who Made Ninja Turtle an Expediter? That Person Needs to Be Slapped

Ninja Turtle has taken on the role of expediter, and I've made every effort to assist her by clearly outlining what needs to be done. However, it's difficult to help someone who lacks the common sense to think independently and is unwilling to put in the effort to learn. Ninja Turtle and some others seem to believe that because Gothic and I work diligently without needing direction, they can simply relax and bring their team to the expediter's desk for casual conversations, expecting everything to run smoothly. In reality, Ninja Turtle often spends over an hour and a half standing in one spot chatting, while the responsibilities fall squarely on Gothic and me.

With her lack of knowledge and management's misunderstanding of the expediter's role, they only take action when they receive a negative email, reacting only after issues arise. Although Ninja Turtle was appointed as the B-section expediter, management seems to rely solely on her input, unaware of the responsibilities that come with the position. What happens when the expediter is unprofessional and oblivious to her duties? It's a classic case of the blind leading the blind.

For example, supervisors and MDOs frequently approach Gothic and me, complaining that we aren't scanning. Despite our reassurances that we are indeed scanning, they continue to insist otherwise. At one point, I found myself subtly questioning, "Are you sure she knows what she's doing?" While I'm not an expert in expediting, I have worked alongside several expediters and am familiar with the standard procedure: get up from the desk, go to the truck, scan the barcode, sit back down, and repeat this process throughout the night. However, Ninja Turtle rarely gets up, which raises red flags; it's evident that something isn't being checked in or out, deviating from the usual expediter routine.

The situation has become so dire that supervisors and managers have begun closely monitoring us to ensure we're scanning. Their focus is misplaced, as the real issue lies with Ninja Turtle. If she were fulfilling her role effectively, and if the supervisors were competent, they would check the system and realize that she wasn't entering the trucks properly. Without her completing this crucial task, our scans will never register, no matter how hard we work.

It's frustrating to be scapegoated for issues that stem from others' negligence. When things go awry, it feels as though we become targets for blame due to the lack of work ethic displayed by those around us. This has led to Ninja Turtle and some of her expediter colleagues adopting a condescending tone, treating us as if they were our supervisors. I refuse to tolerate this behavior, and when they cross that line, I speak up. While they may not appreciate my candor, I believe it's important for them to hear it.

Currently, there's increasing pressure on Ninja Turtle, and it's clear that she doesn't fully grasp what's going wrong, likely due to inadequate training and her reluctance to ask the necessary questions to learn. She sees Gothic and me working hard and assumes we can handle everything, but we are not equipped to do her job. It's not within our training or our union's rules, and we lack the access to perform her duties. Now, every time she starts barking orders, it seems to attract unwanted attention, especially when anyone shows aggression toward Gothic and me.

CHAPTER 44

Miserable Turtle

Ninja Turtle is undeniably unhappy. While this may sound harsh, it's an honest observation. Those who belittle others often suffer internally. In acknowledging her misery, I must also confront my own as I express these thoughts. Seeing the world through my eyes might help you understand the pain of working in an environment that mistreats, stresses, and abuses its employees.

I recognize misery because I speak from experience. As Ninja Turtle approaches 40, she naturally reflects on life, especially as friends settle down, marry, or have children. She longs for someone to call her own, to hold her, or to say, "You are my baby." This connection remains elusive, especially as those around her seem to find it, leading to feelings of sadness and depression.

In a group of friends, not being particularly attractive can result in feeling overlooked. Watching others appear happy or seeing couples share peaceful moments can be irritating when one lacks similar experiences. What gives them the right to be happy after all they've endured? To draw attention, she creates drama, often involving

Gothic and me, and spreads word of conflicts throughout the building. This gives her a sense of clout and the attention she craves.

CHAPTER 45

Batman and the Ninja Turtle: Heroes Work Here

When seeking to uncover hidden adversaries, take a moment to survey your surroundings during any conflict or confrontation. Notice who aligns themselves with the individual you've clashed with; their presence may reveal more than you initially perceive. I was surprised when Batman and I got into it, and he found out I was not what he expected. I noticed that the Ninja Turtle was extra friendly toward him. She talked to him more than usual. I started to notice that she was aligning herself with anyone who was against me. It became a pattern where people were going out of their way just to have an issue with me or Gothic to belong to the Wolfpack and hyena crew.

The Ninja Turtle obviously felt some kind of way because she noticed that I was not going to sit back and allow her to throw me under the bus when she messed up. I'm not going to allow her to delegate tasks to me when we have people sitting around doing nothing but disappearing. She's not my supervisor, and I don't know why she feels like she is. If you want to be my supervisor, you first need to learn how to do your job and do it well before transitioning to something bigger. But since you haven't even passed the bare minimum test of knowing your tasks, I'm not going to let you throw me under the bus or speak to me in a condescending way when you don't know what you're doing.

CHAPTER 46

Miss Gaylord Has Nothing Better to Do

Here we go again with this miserable, ninja turtle-looking woman. I have never had a person obsess over me so much that I once had to call Supervisor Naij to ask if Ninja Turtle had a crush on me or something because I was confused about her obsession. Supervisor Naij told me that she didn't think Ninja Turtle liked me. She could've fooled me because usually if I don't like somebody, I stay away from them. I don't even want to look in their direction. I don't want to hear anything about them. I just want them to not be physically, mentally, or emotionally around me at all. But it seems to be the opposite for this weird chick, Ninja Turtle.

It got to a point where she started to involve other supervisors. I remember one day when Gothic and I were going on break. As soon as we made a quick right, I saw the Ninja Turtle and Miss Gaylord talking out of the corner of my eye. I turned quickly to confirm that they were indeed talking. I turned back and told Gothic what was going on behind us. I knew that something was about to pop off soon because every time something happened and people started gathering behind us, knowing that the person she was talking to was a supervisor, I knew they would try to come after us. I mentioned this to Gothic.

When we came back to the platform after our 15-minute break, it wasn't long before I saw Miss Gaylord sniffing around. I like to be on the offense instead of the defense, so I asked her if she needed help with anything since she was in a place she usually never came to. Something must have drawn her there by our sitting area. She told me that she needed some boxes moved, the boxes that had been in front of where we were sitting before we got there. I simply lined them up to block myself from being harassed. I entertained her by helping her move the boxes, and after I finished, she told me she was going to get someone to come move some broken equipment lined up on the side of where we were sitting.

Coincidentally, Purple came to Gothic and me and asked us to help her work at the line that night. We grabbed our stuff and headed to the line. When I got to the line, I realized I had forgotten something and had to head back to the platform to grab it. When I got to the platform, guess who I saw talking to the Ninja Turtle? I saw Miss Gaylord talking to her while pointing at Gothic and our sitting area. I overheard Miss Gaylord say, "I am going to have someone pick them up." They both started smiling, and I ended up going **back** to the line to let Gothic know **what** I **had** just overheard.

What's wild is that Miss Gaylord and I used to be cool in that every time we crossed paths, we greeted each other. I even asked her at one point why she always wore the color hair she did because it wasn't a typical color that people usually choose and wear every day. Since I've known her, she always wore the same bright-colored hair. When I asked her why, she said it was her favorite color and mentioned something about the ravens. But because the Ninja Turtle got in her ear and because she was cool with Lips (who is no longer here), she felt the best thing to do at that moment was to harass me and Gothic.

Not wanting it to fester, I had to nip it in the bud. I let supervisor Naija know what was going on and asked her to talk to Miss Gaylord because she was going out of her way to target and bother us. How do you leave your busy operation to come to the platform and worry about things that have nothing to do with your operation, nor do you need anything from the platform at that moment? All the equipment and Gaylords over there were either broken or unusable, meaning they needed to be trashed or fixed.

At this point, since people had heard about the issue with Lips and us and how far we were going to fight for our rights, Miss Gaylord backed off after Supervisor Naija talked to her. I think I sent a text or an email about the situation to Supervisor Naija, hoping she could give it to Miss Gaylord to read to see how serious I was about what I was saying because I wouldn't hesitate to file paperwork on her for purposely trying to harass and disturb us.

After that situation, Miss Gaylord left us alone, and when she saw me, she didn't talk to me at all. She has a phony smile on her face. The reason we nicknamed her Miss Gaylord was that she left her busy operation to come to arrange torn, unusable Gaylords and equipment.

CHAPTER 47

Dust Cuz

Dust Cuz is an intriguing individual. Initially, I thought he possessed common sense, unlike many others at the USPS Plantation. We developed a camaraderie through mutual friends, exchanging a fist bump when we met. However, a comment he made one day altered my perception, leading me to limit our interactions. Trust is crucial, and engaging with someone you don't trust can be risky. It's wiser to invest energy in something positive rather than constantly looking over your shoulder.

On that day, Dust Cuz unexpectedly left his work area to ask me, "Who are you trying to impress?" I was taken aback and replied, "What do you mean?" He questioned why I wore my "good clothes" to work. Surprised, I explained, "I'm trying to impress myself. These aren't my good clothes; my suits and button-ups are." I pointed out that his shoes probably cost more than my entire outfit. The clothes he deemed "good clothes" were simply my standard work attire.

As someone who reflects deeply, I pondered why Dust Cuz felt compelled to comment on my appearance. It seemed odd for him to focus on how I dressed, especially since we're both straight men. The only plausible reason for a man to fixate on another's appearance is competition for the same woman. Perhaps he overheard a compliment directed at me, triggering his insecurity. His attempt to make me self-conscious about my attire seemed driven by his discomfort. However, I want him to know that I don't need to try to look good; I can wear almost anything and still carry it well. My background in professional modeling and staying in shape helps clothes look good on me. Instead of fixating on me, he should focus on his own appearance, perhaps by hitting the gym.

Attracting women has never been an issue for me. I follow the rule of not acknowledging other men when they're with women to avoid making them feel insecure. I've had instances where friends introduced me to someone, only to later hear that the woman was interested in me. This has happened multiple times, prompting me to maintain distance to avoid unnecessary drama.

My unique perspective, influenced by autistic traits, allows me to view situations from multiple angles. I often ask myself questions to understand scenarios better. Another peculiar interaction with Dust Cuz occurred after speaking with a Nigerian coworker. Dust Cuz approached me, questioning why I talked to him, implying he was gay. I didn't believe it, as the coworker never raised any suspicions. Regardless of his orientation, mutual respect is what matters to me.

About a year later, Dust Cuz randomly informed me that Gothic used to be "big." This comment caught me off guard, and I replied, "Good for her." Having lost weight myself, I wondered about his motive for sharing this information. Perhaps he had feelings for Gothic and wanted to dissuade me from interacting with her. People often behave strangely when they perceive someone as a competition.

My suspicions were confirmed when another person asked about my relationship with Gothic, prompting me to set boundaries. I made it clear that I don't discuss personal matters and found the question disrespectful. The individual apologized and has since been cautious around me.

Dust Cuz eventually became the B-section expediter after Ninja Turtle moved on. I aimed to help him understand his responsibilities, even texting him details. However, his lazy attitude frustrated me, as he expected Gothic and me to handle everything while he slacked off.

Despite this, I respected him for defending us when Pastor accused us of being lazy. He acknowledged our hard work while others slacked. However, as Supervisor Purple and others made our work environment unbearable, I decided to only fulfill my duties. When he asked for favors, I declined, saying, "Bro, it's not my job." He didn't appreciate this, and I explained that I couldn't take on extra responsibilities when others weren't contributing.

For my well-being, I needed to say no. This upset him, leading him to align with the "Hyena Club," a group of gossipers making our work more challenging. It's baffling that he thinks it's acceptable to act this way towards Gothic and me when we outwork everyone on the platform.

I wish others could experience our workload for a day and reflect on the treatment we receive. It's disheartening to see management's abuse continue because we fail to speak up. If we collectively advocated for fair treatment, significant change could occur. I don't mind working hard, but I won't tolerate mistreatment. Dust Cuz's newfound socializing with supervisors to undermine us is especially frustrating, as those close to him start picking on us for no reason.

CHAPTER 48

Humpty Dumpty and His Best Friend Mr. Black

Humpty Dumpty is one of our regular truck drivers, and we nicknamed him that because he resembles the character in human form. If you can imagine what Humpty Dumpty would look like as a person, that's exactly how this driver appears. Before Humpty Dumpty took over this route, it was driven by a massive man named Mr. Black. When I say "massive," I mean he stands about 6'2" and weighs at least 300 pounds. Mr. Black was always laid back; he would come in, stand in the corner with his shades on, and keep a low profile.

Being naturally observant of my surroundings, I began to notice Mr Black's behavior. After watching him for a while, it became clear that he was soliciting girls for sex. He always carried a lot of cash and would count it when women were around. The way he interacted with certain people made me suspect he was buying sex. My suspicions were confirmed one day when I witnessed him discreetly sliding money to a young lady. The exchange was so secretive that it felt more like a drug deal than anything else.

To verify my observations, I turned to Two-Face, who is known for talking a lot and having plenty of information. Later that night, I asked him, "Hey, quick question. I saw some weird stuff today that made me curious: do you know if there are people buying or selling sex among Postal employees?" Without missing a beat, he replied, "Hell yeah. A lot of these drivers are buying pussy." He went on to express his confusion over why they would pay for something that should be free, mentioning that the two biggest buyers of sex were Mr. Black and his best friend, Humpty Dumpty.

Mr. Black had started setting up something akin to a rat trap. He would intentionally drop money on the floor to attract a young lady's attention. I had seen him do this a few times. One day, feeling that the situation was ridiculous and that we shouldn't have to work in such an environment, I decided to have a little fun. I mentioned that I had previously spoken to my supervisor about this issue and had recently sent an email to management, including several individuals with MDO titles, plant managers, and supervisors. I CCed at least four people in management about this situation, yet not one replied, which underscored the indifference of our management. With that in mind, I decided to play a prank on Mr. Black. He was going through his usual routine, scoping the area from the corner, when I approached him and asked if he had heard about the investigation. Instantly, he became alert and interested. "What investigation?" he asked. I replied, "There's a big investigation into a prostitution ring at Postal. They're looking at employees and drivers." The look on his face was priceless; you would have sworn he had seen a ghost. I asked him again if he had heard anything about it. "No, no, no, I didn't hear anything. Where did you hear that?" he inquired. I could barely contain my laughter at how serious and scared he looked. After I revealed that it was just a joke, we both laughed, and he admitted that I had him scared to death. Then, in a moment of levity, he pulled out a wad of cash and asked, “Do you want me to buy you some hoes?” I chuckled and replied, “I don’t need to pay for sex, my friend. I’ve been blessed not to have to.”

After an incident involving Mr. Black, his best friend, Humpty Dumpty, took over his route. Humpty Dumpty is one of those men who always seems angry and loves to argue. When he walks into the building, you can hear people muttering, “Oh Lord, here he goes again. Not him; he has a bad attitude. What’s he going to complain about today?” He radiates a negative vibe that signals trouble, and people brace themselves for his complaints. Before taking over Mr Black’s route, he would occasionally come by to drop off loads, and rumors swirled that people were afraid of him because he had sued Postal or reported someone who subsequently got fired. Management usually kept their distance from him out of fear.

While I’ve never had any direct issues with him, I can sense a vibe that doesn’t sit well with me. I’m someone who reads energy, and the energy he exudes suggests he doesn’t particularly like me, though I’m not sure why. You know that feeling when someone looks you up and down every time you see them? That’s the impression I get from him. Yet, we’ve never had any confrontations until I had a run-in with Ninja Turtle. That incident made it clear to me that Humpty Dumpty did not like me. I had done nothing to provoke this animosity, yet he seemed willing to wage war against me for no apparent reason. This led me to question, “Why would someone I’ve never had an issue with suddenly turn against me?”

I also find myself pondering the dynamics between two individuals who look so much alike they could pass as father and daughter. Both are short and stocky, but their approaches to relationships are starkly different: one struggles to attract attention from women, so he pays for it, while the other goes above and beyond to draw attention from men. I'm starting to wonder if there's something deeper going on between them or if he is trying to get closer to her. My mind is racing with possibilities as I continue to process this situation.

CHAPTER 49

The Clash with Ninja Turtle

Ninja Turtle clearly craves attention; she simply can't resist being around us, meddling in our work, or constantly talking about us. Gothic and I have essentially dominated her life at this point, and her obsession has only intensified. After enduring relentless harassment, we relocated to a spot where no one seemed to care about us until we settled there. Now, we've become the center of attention in this area.

Ninja Turtle, known for neglecting her responsibilities, decided to disrupt our space by moving all the mail in front of us. The time she spent rearranging the mail could have been better used on more productive tasks, like scanning items or just minding her own business. Unfortunately, this lonely, miserable woman had other plans.

When we arrive, we typically drop our bags and assess what needs our immediate attention. With incoming mail scattered across the platform, we noticed it was mixed with outgoing mail. Gothic and I took the initiative to organize everything, collecting all outgoing mail, such as the various containers destined for Phoenix, and placing them in one designated area. This way, when the driver arrived, they would know exactly where to find it instead of sifting through chaos.

After spending over an hour sorting through the mess, we were surprised to hear someone calling us to put the mail where it was supposed to go. However, there was no space in the designated area, which was precisely why we had organized it that way. Since she began working in the B section, she has never raised concerns about our task management. We excel at this, and the drivers appreciate our efforts. Whenever we're not at work, the disorganization becomes evident, and drivers frequently complain. Yet, despite this, she chose to interfere and instruct us to do something counterproductive.

If we followed her directive and moved the organized mail, it would inevitably mix with incoming items, leading to further chaos. At that moment, we were dealing with individuals who struggled to read the mail, making it even more challenging to determine where items should go if the placards fell off.

The most sensible approach would have been to let us continue our work, as we always have, without issues. So why, all of a sudden, does she feel the need to direct us? Her focus was misplaced; we had more pressing matters that needed our attention.

Recognizing that she was simply trying to provoke us, we chose to ignore her. First, she moved the items we had blocked in our area just to ensure everyone could see us and harass us further. Then, she went to Supervisor Purple to complain. However, Purple saw right through her. She knew who truly ran the platform and recognized our competence. When Supervisor Purple asked us for clarification, we explained why her actions were counterproductive, emphasizing that her interference would only complicate our work and lead to missed packages.

Frustrated that her attempts to reprimand us had failed, Ninja Turtle began hovering around us, speaking loudly enough for Gothic and me to hear. Later, while we were offloading a truck, she approached and said something to which I responded. What followed was a full-blown outburst; she started screaming and cursing at me, prompting Supervisor Purple and MDO Brownie to step in and try to control her.

It's worth noting that she had previously attempted to physically confront me, and if it hadn't been for Gothic intervening, she might have succeeded. Even with the supervisors present, she continued her tirade. I just needed to ensure she didn't lay a hand on me; the noise was merely that, noise. I eventually told Ninja Turtle to grow up, as her childish antics were unwarranted.

Humpty Dumpty, who had been silent throughout the ordeal, only began to act upset after I told Ninja Turtle to grow up and walked away. He huffed and puffed, trying to intimidate me, which only made the supervisors more nervous. However, I want to make it clear: I'm not afraid of anyone in that building. I can handle myself perfectly well, and I wasn't intimidated by anyone there. At least Supervisor Purple was still on our side.

During our lunch break, I spotted Ninja Turtle, Pastor, and Humpty Dumpty in conversation, and I sensed trouble brewing. After we returned from lunch, it wasn't long before Purple approached us, requesting a statement from Gothic because Ninja Turtle was filing a complaint against her, claiming that Gothic had shoved her. We were baffled; how could the aggressor now portray herself as the victim? Clearly, this young woman isn't the sharpest tool in the shed.

CHAPTER 50

Why Must I Endure This Abuse at Work?

Each of us carries a life beyond the walls of USPS, a life filled with dreams, responsibilities, and love. Yet here I am, trapped in a cycle of harassment, bullying, and emotional torment, all while striving to earn a living for my family. It feels unbearably unjust, not just to me but to those I care about. My work life has become a shadow looming over my spirit, dragging me into despair. I am willing to work tirelessly, yet the fruits of my labor are tainted by the poison of mistreatment.

Can management at USPS truly understand the storms raging in my personal life? I doubt it. If they paused to look deeper, they would see the chaos enveloping me. My existence is a whirlwind, a tempest of heartache intertwined with fleeting moments of joy. It's a paradox where I can feel elated yet completely isolated. Loneliness has become a constant companion, creeping into my heart until I grow accustomed to its cold embrace. I ask myself, why do I feel this way? I shouldn't have to bear this burden.

In those moments of solitude, a profound question arises: "Why are they targeting me?" Deep down, I know I am a good person, striving to make life easier for others. I pour my heart into my work every night, giving it my all. So why must I endure this? I do not deserve this torment. Then, like a flash of lightning in the dark, it strikes me: I am greater than this.

I recall conversations with 34X34, reminiscing about the times we were close. I voiced my frustrations about the relentless abuse inflicted by management. 34X34's words echo in my mind: "USPS will never change." Ellen echoed the same sentiment. I once believed change was possible, but that hope now flickers dimly, like a candle struggling against the wind.

In an effort to escape this suffocating reality, I turned to my passion, scriptwriting and filmmaking. But how can creativity flourish in the face of relentless oppression? The abuse of power by USPS management stifles my spirit, preventing me from focusing on what I love. I refuse to be a silent bystander while this injustice unfolds, affecting not only me but also countless dedicated coworkers who deserve better.

In a twisted way, I owe a strange gratitude to USPS management for compelling me to confront my ADHD and pushing me to pen this very book. Each time my focus wavers, their actions ignite a fire within me, compelling me to write. It feels as though the universe has placed me here for a reason: to be a catalyst for change. I am ready to fight, even if it costs me my job. This cycle of abuse must end; it is a burden too heavy to bear.

Together, we must rise as one, united in our struggle against the tyranny of management, against abuse, harassment, and bullying. We owe it to ourselves, to each other, and to the future we deserve. It is time to reclaim our dignity. It is time to say enough is enough.

CHAPTER 51

Ninja Turtle Pressing Charges

How is it possible that Ninja Turtle attempted to physically attack me? She lunged at me, prompting Gothic to create a barrier with her hand. This same young woman, who lost control and cursed me out, had MDO Brownie and Supervisor Purple present, trying to calm her down. The chaos she created drew people away from their sections and disrupted operations, making it difficult for anyone to refocus on their tasks. Such disorder impacts mail movement and ultimately causes delays.

After the incident, it seemed some believed Supervisor Purple should have backed Ninja Turtle. I found it hard to believe that Purple could defend her after such a spectacle. All she did was tell Ninja Turtle to cool off, which only upset Humpty Dumpty, who wanted Purple to side with Ninja Turtle despite her clear wrongdoing.

I suspect that's why Purple asked Gothic to write a statement; it was evident that Ninja Turtle was trying to stir up trouble. Ironically, on the same day they called Gothic into the office for statements, the hyenas in the A section laughed and watched me, completely unaware that I had assessed the situation and was already planning my next move. They weren't as sharp as they thought. I reached out to Purple for the documents I needed to file a report against Ninja Turtle. I was baffled that she nearly attacked me while Gothic intervened; had she not stepped in, someone could have been seriously hurt. Somehow, Ninja Turtle and her crew believed it was appropriate to file a report against Gothic, viewing her as the victim.

I contacted Purple for paperwork regarding Ninja Turtle, and since we had a good rapport, she agreed it made sense for me to file a report. She expressed disbelief that Ninja Turtle would even consider making a report when she was the aggressor.

Yet, they seemed to overlook the fact that Ninja Turtle had almost attacked me and verbally abused me right in front of both supervisors and MDOs. I had witnesses. I knew that if I didn't take action, they would make Gothic's life miserable and possibly fire her just to get at me. That's why it was crucial for me to advocate for that report; it was unfair how they were treating Gothic. Both MDO Brownie and Supervisor Purple witnessed everything, so I wrote a detailed statement and submitted it.

Thanks to the pressure I applied and the contents of my statement, they ultimately chose not to take action against Gothic. You can't justify firing her for stopping an attack while allowing the aggressor to go unpunished. It's outrageous that Miss Has Spoken lost her job and was escorted off the property for something far less severe than what Ninja Turtle did. How is it fair that a woman lost her job after eight years for a minor infraction compared to Ninja Turtle's behavior?

Someone likely advised Ninja Turtle to let this case go, warning her that I would fight back until she faced the consequences for her actions, which were far worse than anything she claimed Gothic did. Ninja Turtle craved attention and thought dragging my name or Gothics into the mix would help. She went around the building recounting the incident, and when she saw us, she felt the need to acknowledge us with loud noises or laughter, completely oblivious to the fact that we didn't care about her antics. Yet, she dedicates so much energy to us that she often loses her composure in the process.

Sometimes, when she spots us, she starts talking loudly. One day, as Gothic and I were walking to our break, we noticed her from across the way. As soon as she saw us, she stopped and walked toward us, seemingly trying to draw attention. One of her friends asked, "When are you going back to the platform?" to which she replied, "Never because I know about that drama," all while looking at us as we walked past. The young woman seems genuinely miserable and lonely. When we sit outside on break, we can see her inside, and when she's alone, she appears utterly desolate, searching for attention but unable to find it without being excessively loud.

CHAPTER 52

They Love Our Presence

Ninja Turtle seems unable to leave us alone since she stopped being an expediter on the platform. She has returned to her position inside the building, which is quite far from our workspace. Ideally, we could spend the entire night without crossing paths, except in common areas like the break room or the bathroom. However, for some reason, she now feels the need to come to the platform, not just for a visit, but specifically to the B section. She speaks loudly and makes provocative comments, seemingly trying to elicit a reaction from us and draw attention to herself.

Rather than engaging with her, I decided to report the situation to my supervisors. I know how these dynamics often unfold; if I confront her, I'll likely be seen as the aggressor. I prefer to address any issues directly with my management. Unfortunately, nothing usually comes of it since they tend to side with Ninja Turtle. Each time she approaches the B section, she indirectly references us, laughing loudly for no apparent reason.

Whenever she shows up, I make it a point to inform my supervisor about what's happening and to inquire about the status of my case against her. I approached Brownie, my MDO, and then my supervisor, but it felt like I was going in circles. Brownie would send me back to my supervisor, claiming it was her responsibility to handle the paperwork and vice versa.

Eventually, I contacted the Union and learned they were waiting for paperwork from either my supervisor or MDO Brownie. As I increased my pressure regarding the case, I noticed Ninja Turtle stopped coming to the B section altogether and began hanging around the A section with the Hyena group, watching us work. I can't understand how eight people can gather, chatting while all facing us, laughing loudly in an attempt to catch our attention. I've learned that if someone is that desperate for my attention, I'll act as if they don't exist. Gothic and I often see how loud we can get them by completely ignoring them and pretending to have an engaging conversation, which usually prompts them to get louder until they tire of it.

Unfortunately, they don't seem to lose interest. The situation escalated to the point where we started joking among ourselves, saying things like, "Damn, my aura must be so great that they can't help but talk about us," or "I should start signing autographs because I feel like a top-tier Hollywood actor with the way they're watching my every move." It's disconcerting to be so acutely aware of their eyes on us, worrying about making a mistake and fearing their laughter. It felt as if they wanted to get so close they could smell our perfume or cologne, even going so far as to jump over barricades for a better look.

One day, I caught one of the Hyenas filming Gothic. It was the strangest thing I'd ever seen. As I returned from loading something onto the truck, I noticed a Hyena member on a forklift inching closer to where Gothic was sitting. I saw her phone go up, and she slowed down, aiming it as if trying to capture something. When I got closer, I asked, "Why are you recording her?" She quickly shut off her phone and drove away. I immediately reported the incident to Supervisor Purple. She remarked that they were being childish and suggested I record her back. I thought, "I don't think we're allowed to record anything on this property, especially since it's federal land and we handle people's packages containing sensitive information." It surprised me to hear a supervisor suggest such an action.

I also reported the incident to the Union but discovered that the Union Rep was close to that particular Hyena member. Realizing it wouldn't be beneficial to escalate things further, I decided to take a different approach. I told the Union Rep that I would contact the inspectors to see how they felt about recording on the property. When I asked her if recording people here was allowed, she said no and shared some rules and regulations. I mentioned that I would reach out to the inspectors to see if they could pull the footage and investigate the recording incident.

As I mentioned earlier, I know Union members gossip, and if I told this Union Rep (whom I nicknamed Cushion) about the incident, she would likely spread the word. At this point, no one is discussing Ninja Turtle's case against Gothic; it is silent as a mouse. However, I kept pressing management to address the situation, but I continued to receive the same back-and-forth responses. Ninja Turtle no longer came to the B section; instead, she stood in the A section with the Hyenas, laughing. Every time we walked past her, she made comments.

For instance, one day, it was almost time to leave, and Ninja Turtle and her friends were near the main time clock area where we swipe our badges. Rather than waiting there, we decided to walk a little further to another station with a time clock. Since we clocked in early and had a five-minute grace period, we swiped our badges and took the quickest route to the front door. As we first walked past Ninja Turtle and her crew, they chuckled and laughed, but we didn't care. When we finished clocking out and headed toward them again to exit the building, they were now facing us as we approached.

One thing I won't do is avoid making eye contact. As we walked toward them, they looked at us, but as we got closer, they couldn't maintain eye contact, likely out of fear or insecurity. Just as we passed them, Ninja Turtle remarked to her crew, "They could've just walked around," implying we should have taken the longer route to the exit. After working hard for eight hours, I'm not going to take extra steps for anyone. Why were they standing in such a high-traffic area if they didn't want to be noticed? I'm not changing my route for anyone. I'm professional enough to handle myself, but if they want to be noticed, I won't complicate my job by walking all the way around the building to leave. Instead of suggesting, "Why don't they walk around?" she should have thought about moving out of the way so people could pass and go home.

CHAPTER 53

Purple Was Forced to Cave to the Wolfpack and the Hyena Club

I began to notice a change in Supervisor Purple; it was evident that she was under immense pressure. Her movements became less assured, her smile no longer felt genuine, and her energy visibly waned. It seemed as though the constant scrutiny from the Wolfpack and the Hyena Club, particularly regarding Gothic and me sitting in the area marked with the "Do Not Block" sign, was wearing her down. One day, Purple approached us, expressing her confusion over their fixation on that small space and our presence there.

"Do me a favor; please make sure you clean up this area and move all the boxes before you go on your 30-minute break," she said. We typically took our break at 4:30 PM, with leadership trickling in starting around 5 AM until we finished at 6:30 AM. To ease

Purple's mind, I offered to take a video and pictures of the "DO NOT BLOCK" area where Gothic and I sat after cleaning it up. This way, the other supervisors from different shifts couldn't claim we left a mess. Purple loved the idea, and that's what we did.

By documenting the area as evidence of our cleanup, I could easily show Purple how it looked when we arrived after cleaning the previous day. This demonstrated that others had occupied the space when we weren't there, and during other shifts, no one had said a word about the mess left behind. Yet, when Gothic and I occupied the area, it became an issue, making it seem as if we were responsible for the mess when, in fact, we were the ones cleaning up after others.

Due to Supervisor Purple treating us better than previous management, 34X34 grew angry. I began to hear her speak negatively about Purple as if she were a bad supervisor. She shared her thoughts with coworkers and truck drivers. Things were improving for us because, for the first time, we had a supervisor who genuinely looked out for our best interests and acknowledged that we were not the problem. Her verbal reassurances led to better attendance, increased happiness, and more smiles all around. This did not sit well with others; our happiness seemed to threaten their misery. As we became slightly happier, they grew resentful, blaming Supervisor Purple for their unhappiness.

I noticed many of them began calling off work, including the expediters and some of my coworkers. Since Purple's office was right by the A section, I assumed she overheard many negative comments about her while there. This might explain why she often mentioned needing a vacation. It was clear to me that she was being attacked from all angles by the Wolfpack and the Hyena crew, who were determined to break her spirit. Upon reflection, it made sense why Supervisor Naij had told me she didn't want it to seem like we were close, even though we were from the same country. She isolated herself from me and treated me worse than those she wasn't close to.

CHAPTER 54

Zero Tolerance

Things are starting to get out of hand. Ninja Turtle remains miserable and desperate for attention, laughing loudly and making comments designed to provoke a reaction. The situation is escalating toward a physical confrontation. One day, as Gothic and I were leaving the building, we approached the last door and saw Ninja Turtle standing in front of it, blocking our exit as the door slowly closed. It was moving so slowly that we could have reached it before it shut.

As we neared the door, Ninja Turtle watched us and slammed it shut just as we reached for it. It seemed she had been waiting outside, though I couldn't tell if it was specifically for Gothic and me or if she was just there. Regardless, her action made little sense unless it was meant to provoke us. She had no reason to touch that door since she was already outside. The only motive for her actions was to slam it in our faces, unaware that someone could get hurt in the process. Management was informed about the incident, and it was included in an email sent to several people in charge. Since she didn't physically harm us, we decided not to engage with Ninja Turtle, denying her the satisfaction of a reaction, which is what she craves. Gothic and I acted as if we hadn't noticed her actions, simply getting in the car and driving away.

This unhappy Ninja Turtle can't seem to leave us alone. It feels like we've taken over her life, given how much she thinks about us and plans her day around our presence, while we just want to distance ourselves from her toxic energy. For a few days, she began appearing in the B section of the platform. We resolved to remain silent, hoping our complete indifference would communicate that she didn't exist to us.

When she came to the B section, she would start talking to others, purposefully trying to be loud and obnoxious in hopes of provoking a reaction from us. However, we weren't going to give her that satisfaction. Wearing headphones and pretending to be engrossed in our phones made it easy to ignore her. I think this frustrated her because she made multiple appearances each night, growing louder with each visit. We could hear her, but we had no intention of acknowledging someone so miserable who thrived on attention from those who clearly didn't care about her.

Even while on my phone, I remained aware of my surroundings and noticed her looking at us several times, searching for a response. It was time for us to load the Metro truck, and as we went back and forth through the same doors with equipment, often requiring around 24 BMCs to fill the truck, Ninja Turtle's next move infuriated me. She timed it perfectly so that, as we turned left to exit after returning from our 15-minute break, she came out of nowhere and shoulder-bumped Gothic. What is wrong with this girl? Why can't she leave us alone? Doesn't she have anyone else to entertain her?

Then it hit me: who would want to be around someone so lonely and filled with negativity? After this incident, we waited about two to three hours until Purple returned to the platform. When I saw her, I informed her about the encounter and reminded her of the previous door-slamming incident with Ninja Turtle.

While walking to the bathroom, I noticed Purple talking to Ninja Turtle. By the end of our shift, Gothic was called to the general clerk's office. As she headed there, I decided to take my 15-minute break. We speculated about the reason for her being called in and ended up running into a group blocking our path. Someone from the group said they were going to learn about zero tolerance today. I didn't understand it until Gothic returned from the office.

The story is about Miss Butterfly, who is in the office, and they discuss the incident between Gothic and Ninja Turtle. They lectured her about the zero-tolerance policy, and Gothic provided a statement for the subsequent investigation. A day or two later, Gothic was called back into the office in the middle of her shift and was sent home with instructions not to return until further notice. Within three days, she received paperwork informing her to come back to work, effectively suspending her for something she did not provoke or instigate.

I started processing the entire situation, my mind racing to make sense of it all. I wanted to find out where Supervisor Purple was, so I approached her and asked why Gothic had been called into the office and why they were trying to portray her as the aggressor when I had reported the incident first. They were aware of the previous events, including the door-slamming situation. Why was Gothic being punished for something she didn't do? It didn't seem right.

I wanted to gauge Purple's response to see if she was involved in Gothic's troubles. However, the way she began to speak made me sense her involvement in the situation, leading to Gothic's suspension. Everything is in the eyes. If you frequently talk to someone and they maintain eye contact but suddenly avoid it, they are likely hiding something. That's exactly what I sensed from Purple.

I recalled someone from the group saying they were going to learn what zero tolerance was. Was that truly a coincidence, or did someone predict what was about to happen? Did someone from the union, management, or Ninja Turtle leak information that has not yet been released? It seemed like confidential information was being shared, and those directly involved in the altercation had no idea about the outcome. It was as if someone had foreseen Gothic's discussion about zero tolerance. Mind you, none of those people in that group worked on the platform or were present during any incidents, so for them to know this information, it suggested someone was leaking details. It felt like a conspiracy.

It's unfortunate that nothing remains confidential when the union or management hears about it, as they use that information to gossip and stir drama. Instead of keeping things private for the safety of both parties, it seems there will be no more occasions without people creating trouble.

Purple began making excuses, claiming she didn't know anything about it. However, I informed her about Ninja Turtle's supposed report, and as a supervisor, she should have been aware of what had occurred or what was about to happen to one of her employees. I knew she was lying to me, especially since I had just seen her talking to

Ninja Turtle, and it didn't appear to be a casual conversation; it looked serious. I could see the lies in her eyes. That day, I realized that Purple was compromised; the Wolfpack and Hyenas had gotten to her.

CHAPTER 55

Mr. Slick Came Back

I knew Mr. Slick couldn't help himself. He had to come back. Now, he works at a different operation. His stalkerish tendencies are still present, but they seem more controlled, possibly because more people are aware of the unsettling situation that unfolded between him, Gothic, and me. He still finds ways to linger, hovering just on the periphery of our lives, but it's not as pronounced as it once was.

Even though he doesn't work on the platform anymore, he makes his presence felt whenever Gothic is around. He moves mail near whatever truck we're working on or engages with people close to our workspace. What I can't comprehend is why, during these interactions, he always turns his body toward us as if he's magnetically drawn to our every move. Thankfully, compared to before, he is learning to keep his distance, but the discomfort still hangs in the air.

CHAPTER 56

Prayer for Mr. Slick

Dear Lord, I lift up a prayer for Mr. Slick. I ask for your forgiveness for his sins and the hurt he has caused others. I hope he eventually finds peace and happiness. Life can be a heavy burden, and many of us carry our own struggles, yet I cannot fully comprehend the weight he bears. All I know is what he has shared with me, and I pray that the pain he carries is lifted, allowing him to discover true joy.

I pray that he reconnects with his stepdaughter and wife, finding joy in the life we've been given. For the past three years, his actions have made it challenging for Gothic and me to come to work and feel at ease. He has turned many against us, tarnishing our reputations and shattering our sense of tranquility on that property.

Like him, we all face personal battles outside of work. Rather than being a catalyst for further turmoil in our lives, I hope he can become a source of light. I pray that he finds the strength to bring joy to others instead of pain, anger, and tears.

Honestly, I don't know what the future holds, but despite everything he has done to Gothic and me, I still wish him well. I pray for his transformation into someone who spreads happiness rather than sorrow.

And Lord, I want to express my gratitude for bringing Mr. Slick into my life. Without the pain and turmoil he caused, I might have grown too comfortable in my position at the Postal Service, content to stay until retirement. However, because of Mr. Slick and the discomfort he created, I have sought to use my gifts to effect change. I'm determined to make an impact before I leave, knowing that if I remain silent, nothing will change.

Thank you, dear Lord, for everything you have done for me. I hope you sprinkle some happiness into Mr. Slick's life, enabling him to rise above his past and embrace a brighter future.

CHAPTER 57

"DO NOT BLOCK" AREA

Reflecting on the behavior and mindset of those in managerial roles, it becomes increasingly clear that the USPS might struggle to thrive over the next decade. Their priorities seem misaligned, focusing on trivial matters instead of the core mission of ensuring timely mail delivery and maintaining customer satisfaction. It's disheartening to see an emphasis on areas that don't enhance mail movement or facility efficiency.

A glaring example is the area Gothic and I were essentially forced to occupy, marked by a "Do Not Block" sign. This spot, seemingly insignificant, has become the center of attention at the USPS Plantation. Ironically, supervisors and MDOs seem more concerned about this small area, roughly the size of two phone booths, than about more pressing issues. These include the facility's poor Google rating, employees disappearing for hours, unauthorized truck drivers wandering the building, and the general lack of cleanliness and safety. The pungent aroma of weed in the parking lot and the sight of impaired equipment drivers are overlooked, yet this tiny space has become their focus.

Previously unnoticed and littered with trash until we arrived, this area has now sparked significant attention. It had been ignored, but it became a popular spot because

Gothic and I chose to sit there, only to be told not to, with signs posted reading, “This is not a break area. Please do not take your breaks or lunches in this area. Do not block this door. Do not place trays in this area. Do not store cardboard in this area. Do not sit in this area. This area is to remain clear.” Gothic and I joke that if we sat in every corner of the building, the entire place would eventually be spotless, drawing the focus of supervisors and MDOs away from their actual responsibilities.

The situation is increasingly concerning for Purple. The constant scrutiny of this trivial space by colleagues, coupled with the movements of Brownie and Miss Beef Patty, suggests something is afoot. I can’t help but feel a sense of distrust towards them, as they were part of the original Wolfpack. With the departure of the Wolfpack’s queen, her followers are now targeting us, placing immense pressure on Purple. She faces a critical decision: continue to stand her ground or allow the Wolfpack to attack us unchecked.

CHAPTER 58

Damn! Purple's Birthday Is Coming Soon

With Purple's birthday approaching, the anticipation of her taking a week off fills me with dread. For the past month, we've known this day was coming, and her role as a buffer between us and the Wolfpack and hyenas is crucial. Without her, I foresee inevitable attacks, prompting me to devise a strong offense and defense to prepare for any eventuality.

Being naturally analytical, I focus on controlling damage and outcomes. Gothic and I have discussed Purple's upcoming time off extensively, prompting me to prepare strategies. My primary aim was to maintain efficiency on the platform during her absence, ensuring we could operate without disruption.

However, we quickly faced a dilemma. The more we accomplished, the more was expected from us, yet we received less support. While others lounged in their sections, Gothic and I pressed on. Every break we took became contentious. They wanted us to step in as equipment drivers, but instead of using equipment, they expected us to handle tasks manually. We were pulled in every direction while drivers sat idle, forcing me to abandon that plan.

Given how heavily they relied on us, we decided to leverage our work ethic. When attempts were made to overwork us, our only option was to call off. This tactic proved effective, as it typically resulted in reduced pressure on us in the days following. It reached a point where I felt the need to take time off just to find some peace.

Though we lacked sick leave, vacation days, or paid time off, the stress and abuse we endured made it nearly unbearable to go to work. I enjoy physical labor and had to shift my mindset, viewing it as a place that paid me to work out. Each day, I approached it as my gym for the next eight hours.

But unlike a gym, this environment came with mental abuse, which was where I struggled. I don't mind working hard; it's the mental strain, exacerbated by management's mistreatment, that wears me down. As I sit at home before work, dread consumes me. Mentally drained, my body no longer sees this as a gym but as torture. I'm not allowed simply to do my job and go home. My job should not include verbal abuse, harassment, pettiness, or bullying.

Already unhappy with my treatment, I now face colleagues going out of their way to make my work life more stressful. Why can't I just come work, do my job, and earn money to provide for my family? Imagine calling off because you're unable to handle the mental stress awaiting you. Gothic, and I eventually took on side gigs to pay the bills despite having full-time jobs. We feel targeted, suspecting this is a tactic to drive us to quit or call off enough times to justify firing us.

This situation is unfair. We just want to do what we're paid to do: move mail. The job itself isn't the issue; it's everything else: people treating us as if we're beneath them, yelling and cursing. The mental abuse is suffocating.

It's ironic that everyone knows we complete our tasks, yet some overstep boundaries, frustrating us and leading to overwork. How is this fair to those of us who just want to provide for our families? I'm not alone in this struggle. This is why I'm writing this book: to let people know they don't have to endure this. Together, we can speak up and advocate for a better work-life experience.

CHAPTER 59

Here We Go Again, "DO NOT BLOCK" Sitting Area

Here comes a woman shaped like a family-sized, unhealthy cereal box, wobbling down here with her miserable friend, Miss Beef Patty. They approach with their untrustworthy, sinister smiles and a hint of unattractiveness. Why do they stop right in front of our sitting area? Out of this vast property and this platform that stretches as long as a football field, somehow, this is the spot where these two women choose to stand. I can feel that something is about to happen, and I sense it because I'm watching everyone associated with the Wolfpack and hyenas, and they are focused on what these two are doing.

You know how, when watching Animal Planet, you see the lions or wolves preparing to attack their prey while all the other animals watch? That's exactly what's happening right now. Everyone is peeking out to see what's about to unfold, and it makes me uneasy, so I'm alert and assessing the situation. I notice that this cereal box-shaped woman is speaking in a low tone to Miss Beef Patty. Whenever she says something, she leans to the side and sneaks a glance at us from her peripheral vision. You can tell they are up to something. They're bad actresses; their performance is transparent, and it's evident they're not here with good intentions.

When these two women show up, you know something is brewing. I don't trust them at all. From what I've heard from other supervisors, they are not to be trusted; they throw people under the bus and are excessively vicious. The reason I mentioned that Miss Beef Patty doesn't have anything to go home to, no husband, no child, no pet, is because another supervisor shared that information. That's how I know she's miserable in her life outside of USPS Plantation. The supervisor also mentioned that the reason you always see her here stealing time is that she's lonely and unhappy outside of work.

These two ladies are standing in front of where we sit as if they are our bodyguards in the VIP section of a trendy club. Oh no, something is definitely about to happen now because I see purple walking toward us, and all eyes are on her. The sinister smiles from MDO Brownie widen as she calls for Gothic and me, positioning us in front of these three women as if we are about to be lynched or sacrificed. I glance at their faces, struggling to make eye contact with them, which only reinforces my sense that something is about to go very wrong. The person I truly want to make eye contact with is Purple, but the look on her face suggests she feels very uncomfortable.

Do you know how some street gangs require you to perform a violent act to join? Typically, the gang members stand in the background while the person trying to join is in front, about to do something to please them, whether it's committing a crime or enduring a beating. That's the vibe I'm getting from this scene. They are waiting for

Purple to speak, and she begins with, "You guys cannot stay here anymore because you're not supposed to block this door," blah, blah. I can tell she doesn't believe what she's saying; it's clear she's being forced to say it. I can see it written all over her face, and she must feel something tugging at her, telling her she's doing something wrong.

Do you know why she feels conflicted? Because she was the one who told us how unfair it was for management to target us. She was the one who said, "I don't know why this small space is an issue." She was the one who promised to tell them to leave us alone. She was the one who said we were not the problem. She was the one who assured us she would inform us of the days she called off. Of course, she can't make eye contact. Of course, she feels guilty because deep down, she knows what she's doing is wrong. But she stands there reciting her lines as if they were rehearsed, her words coming out robotic and devoid of feeling. It's clear this is something forced upon her, and I can see those two women with their evil grins flanking her.

I try to make my case. I tell them, "Before we started sitting here, other people from different shifts sat there, and if you go check, you'll find cobwebs over there. That lets you know nobody uses that door at all. I've been working here for over four years, and I've never seen anyone use that door. The reason there's all this broken equipment and trash in front of it is that nobody cares about this area." I point out how many times we've moved before coming to this spot, and every place we went seemed to become the target area. "Where else do you want us to go? The roof?" I asked, and she suggested a location, but I reminded her we'd sat there before, and people had issues with us being in that area because it became a storage spot for everyone.

Even though we have a vast area on the platform, whatever space we occupy seems to be prioritized for staging mail. Long story short, they forced us to move from one area to another. I told them that after we moved, I knew it would become an issue again. Brownie insisted they wouldn't bother us if we moved over there. However, once we were relocated, people started coming from their operations to walk past and gawk at us as if it were planned as if we were being targeted. Some walked by smiling and laughing, and I could easily spot those who were out to gloat, like Ninja Turtle, who couldn't help but chuckle as she passed by. Even Mr. Slick walked past a few times with a grin on his face. That day, I felt uncomfortable because I hadn't anticipated such an immediate reaction. I knew it would happen eventually, but I wasn't prepared for it, and I hate feeling unprepared when dealing with these hyenas and the Wolfpack.

When I got home, I began to reflect what had transpired. I tried to identify mistakes and areas where I could have adjusted my approach. I started thinking more about how to prevent myself and Gothic from feeling uncomfortable, as looking or feeling uneasy can make you seem weak and vulnerable. After much thought, I devised a plan and discussed it with Gothic. Our strategy was to sit down in our camping foldable chairs as if we owned the place.

So, the next day, we decided to sit down during downtime and look very comfortable while doing so. When you appear at ease and are engaged in conversation, so immersed that everything around you fades away, that's the impression we wanted to create. Just as I predicted, it became an issue because we looked too comfortable. Knowing I have a bad back is why I brought the camping foldable chairs.

Now, the camping foldable chairs have become a problem. It is documented that I have back issues, but they didn't care about that. The only concern was that we appeared too comfortable and too happy, even after they tried their best to make us uncomfortable. Our comfort and happiness made them uneasy, and now the focus shifted to the camping foldable chairs. I noticed Brownie and MDO Beef Patty walking past a few times since we moved, visibly bothered that we didn't look uncomfortable or upset.

So, they sent their new flunky, the latest official member of the Wolfpack, Supervisor Purple, to confront us. She approaches and says we cannot sit in the camping foldable chairs anymore because they are not USPS-authorized. Now I'm furious because, without this chair, I'll have to increase my medication if I sit on these pallets due to my chronic back pain. I asked her to clarify what she meant by "USPS-authorized chairs." Purple explains it's about liability; in case someone falls, if it's not an authorized chair, they might get sued. I asked if I could get an authorized chair, and she told me no. Then, I point out that everyone in the C-section is sitting in actual chairs with cushions and back support.

When I asked her for one of those chairs, Purple told me they were not supposed to be sitting on those chairs; they had borrowed them from a different operation and had to return them before leaving. I know that's a lie because those chairs have never moved from where they are. But this is where I see through the deception: everything they do is aimed at making us uncomfortable. They aren't as clever as they think; I overanalyze every word spoken to me. I decided to use her words against her and told her that since they're allowed to borrow chairs and return them after their shift, I should be able to do the same.

You'd think that would be checkmate on my part, but guess what? They can adjust the rules and regulations anytime they want. What applies to one person may not apply to another; the rules are murky when dealing with these people. Look at how the rules change: "This is not a sit-down operation." She says no one is supposed to be sitting down, but she will allow us to sit during downtime because standing wouldn't make sense. All I'm asking for is the same treatment they receive. Unlike them, I've documented chronic back pain.

I'm simply asking for the same accommodations they receive. I wouldn't need to bring my chair if they provided me with one like they do in the C-section. Purple knew this was a solid argument, so what she said next was, "I'm going to have them move all the chairs from the C-section." I want you to understand what's happening at this moment. Purple would prefer to remove all the chairs from the C-section, making everyone uncomfortable and upset with her, rather than help someone with serious back issues.

It's no longer about where we sit or what we sit on. This is about making us uncomfortable. When I asked her what I needed to do to use my chair due to my back pain, she told me the only way they'd allow me to have my camping foldable chair was if I got a doctor's note. I went to my doctor, got a note, and handed it to Purple. Now, she tells me I still can't sit down until the plant manager approves it, and that process will take some time. At this point, I'm fed up. "Give me back my paper. I'm tired of this back-and-forth. I'm tired of being picked on. I'm tired of not receiving the same treatment as others. I'm tired of working hard and being mistreated. I'm exhausted from this abuse."

That's exactly what I thought in my mind. So, I asked her nicely to return my paper and walked away to sit on those hard pallets. Then she approached me again, asking if I was sure I didn't want her to take the paper to the plant manager for approval. I wanted to say, "Bitch, get out of my face," because I was already in pain from sitting on these hard pallets. "I'm good," I replied. "Are you sure?" she asked. I thought to myself, "This Bitch is antagonizing me." I chose to ignore her until she left my sight because I had nothing more to say. I realized she was no longer someone I could trust, someone who was supposed to protect her employees, someone I could turn to with complaints.

That was a crushing blow because the one person I thought was on our side did a complete turnaround, leaving us stranded, and now it's causing us to loathe the job even more.

CHAPTER 60

The Wolfpack Pounces

As the clock struck 10 PM, Gothic and I stepped into the USPS Plantation, bracing ourselves for another grueling shift. However, the moment we removed our jackets, an unsettling shift in the atmosphere caught our attention. The usual chatter and idle banter among the A section crew had been replaced by an ominous silence.

Instinctively, I scanned the area, searching for any sign of our supervisor, Purple. To my dismay, she was nowhere to be found. Gothic, sensing my unease, asked the fateful question: "What's today's date?"

My heart sank as the realization hit me, it was the week of Purple's birthday. The Wolfpack and their Hyena cronies had been lying in wait, knowing that with Purple absent, they would have free rein to unleash their wrath upon us.

Sure enough, as we began our work, the vultures started to circle. Their movements were erratic, their gazes fixed. Supervisor Mr. Redshirt hovered nearby, and before long, MDO Brother Man joined him, their presence clearly intended to intimidate us. It was no secret that these two were also known for hitting on female workers.

Gritting my teeth, I turned to the supervisors and firmly requested some personal space, reminding them that I was neither their servant nor their child. The nerve of these individuals, crowding us while we tried to fulfill our duties, only fueled my growing frustration.

Sensing the impending explosion, Gothic and I devised a plan. We would complete our tasks with utmost efficiency, leaving no room for the Wolfpack and Hyenas to find fault. As we worked tirelessly, others were systematically reassigned to areas outside the B section, their absence heightening the tension.

The Hyenas in the A section, sensing their opportunity slipping away, grew increasingly boisterous, their laughter and chatter a cacophony of mockery. But Gothic and I refused to be drawn in, maintaining our focus and productivity, determined to deny them the satisfaction they so desperately craved.

Days passed, and the pressure mounted until an incident occurred that shattered the fragile peace. Team Lead 34X34 approached us with blatant disrespect, snatching a tub from beside us and making disparaging remarks. When I dared to confront her about her unprofessional behavior, she unleashed a torrent of homophobic slurs and personal attacks, all while her Hyena cohorts looked on with glee.

Enough was enough. I knew I needed to document this latest act of harassment to create a paper trail that could no longer be ignored. In a scathing letter, I detailed the incident, the pattern of abuse, and my growing frustration with management's lack of action. This was my line in the sand, a declaration that I would no longer tolerate the Wolfpack's reign of terror.

As I pressed send on the email, I steeled myself for the inevitable backlash. The Wolfpack had been cornered, and I knew they wouldn't go down without a fight. But I was ready, determined to expose their cruelty and demand the respect and dignity that I, along with all my coworkers, deserved.

CHAPTER 61

Are MDO Brownie and 34x34 Related?

As I continued to face relentless abuse and harassment from 34x34, I couldn't shake the feeling that there was more to the situation than met the eye. How could someone with such blatant disregard for her duties as a platform lead maintain her position while my concerns were consistently ignored by management?

I began asking around, hoping to uncover any potential connections that might explain this glaring lack of accountability. The whispers and laughter that followed my inquiries only fueled my suspicions, and there had to be some sort of relationship or protection at play.

Determined to get to the bottom of this, I composed a strongly worded email addressed to MDO Brownie, a higher-up in management. I minced no words, directly confronting the possibility that 34x34 was related to someone in a position of power, which would explain the apparent unwillingness to discipline her.

"If it's true that you are related, it would certainly explain why there seems to be a lack of accountability for her actions," I wrote. I made it clear that I would not stand idly by and allow this abuse to continue, whether it involved 34x34 using derogatory language or engaging in any other form of harassment.

I demanded that 34x34 be terminated, drawing parallels to how I would be swiftly fired if I used similar offensive terms. "If 34x34 is not held to the same standard, I will ensure that the issue is brought to light in a way that cannot be ignored," I warned.

MDO Brownie needed to understand the severity of the situation and the lengths I was willing to go to expose the systemic issues within the USPS Plantation. I made it abundantly clear that I had meticulously documented past incidents and was prepared to risk my own job to stand up against this injustice.

"This is not a threat; it's a promise," I stated firmly. "I expect this case to be handled appropriately, just as it would be if someone used terms like 'faggot' or 'bitch.' I do not deserve this treatment, and I will no longer tolerate disrespect."

The ball was now in MDO Brownie's court. I had laid out my demands and made it clear that I would not back down, even if it meant taking drastic measures to bring the truth to light. The fate of 34x34's employment and the future of the USPS Plantation now rested on how MDO Brownie and the rest of management chose to respond.

CHAPTER 62

I Refuse to Be Ignored

As I continued to face relentless abuse and harassment from 34x34, I knew I could no longer remain silent. The derogatory language she directed at me, including homophobic slurs like "faggot" and "gay," was completely unacceptable, especially given that she herself identified as a lesbian. The blatant hypocrisy of her actions infuriated me.

I had meticulously documented each incident, yet management continually brushed aside my concerns, refusing to hold 34x34 accountable. Enough was enough. I was determined to ensure that this time, my complaints would not be swept under the rug.

Composing a strongly worded email, I addressed it directly to MDO Brownie and MDO Brother Man, copying Supervisor Purple who was currently on vacation. I made it clear that if these matters were not resolved by the following Tuesday, I would have no choice but to escalate my concerns further, including filing a formal complaint and an EEO claim.

"I would like to highlight the unacceptable behavior displayed by 34x34, who has repeatedly directed derogatory remarks towards me," I wrote. I reminded them that this was not an isolated incident, and despite my documentation, management had failed to take appropriate action.

I expressed my continued frustration regarding the incident where a young lady had attempted to physically assault me. I demanded that the necessary documentation be provided, as I was committed to pursuing this matter until it was treated with the seriousness it warranted. "I will not be silenced, nor will I accept being treated as anything less than one of the most dedicated employees in our organization," I stated firmly.

I emphasized management's crucial responsibility to protect all employees from bias and hostility in the workplace. This was not about personal validation; it was about ensuring a safe and respectful work environment for everyone.

The individual who had previously attempted to attack me was continuing to approach the B section, behaving disruptively and provocatively. This created a hostile environment that was simply unacceptable.

Acknowledging potential favoritism within the organization, I made it clear that management must prioritize the well-being of all employees, particularly those who, like myself, were solely focused on their job responsibilities. My case had been mishandled too many times, and I would no longer allow it to be ignored.

"The derogatory comments directed at me directly contradict my values, and although I initially chose to overlook 34x34's behavior, I can no longer remain passive," I stated. "This is just the beginning of my efforts to ensure that my concerns are acknowledged and addressed."

The ball was now firmly in management's court. I had laid out my demands and made it clear that I was prepared to take further action if my complaints were not met with the seriousness they deserved.

CHAPTER 63

How Am I the Aggressor?

As I continued to face relentless abuse and harassment from 34x34, I knew I had to keep the pressure on management to address the situation. It was clear that the pressure was starting to affect them, as evidenced by 34x34's behavior.

Being highly attuned to those around me, I noticed subtle cues that revealed 34x34's true state of mind. When nervous, she bites her fingernails incessantly. When trying to appear unfazed, she crosses her legs in a stiff, almost comical posture, reminiscent of Mr. Peanut from Planters.

The most telling sign is when she blasts music through her headphones and sings loudly, a transparent attempt to convince everyone, including herself, that she's unbothered. Yet, her every fidget and forced nonchalance betray the turmoil she's experiencing.

It's a gift, really, this heightened awareness of mine. I can read people like an open book, their true emotions revealed in the subtle movements of their bodies. In this case, it's clear that 34x34, along with her cohorts Cushion and the Hyena group, has been conspiring against me.

Suddenly, out of nowhere, Supervisor Miss Island approached Gothic, bombarding her with questions. After Gothic relayed the interaction to me, I knew exactly what was happening: they were trying to reframe the narrative to cast me as the aggressor. I refuse to accept that.

Wasting no time, I composed a scathing email addressed directly to MDO Brownie and Supervisor Purple. "I believe this situation may be an attempt to position me as the aggressor to protect 34x34," I wrote with unwavering conviction.

I made it clear that I would not be silenced. "I plan to reach out via mass email to all relevant corporate contacts whose email addresses I can obtain through LinkedIn and Google searches," I declared. "In my message, I will detail how MDO Brownie managed my cases and the injustices I have experienced."

The time for holding back was over. I was determined to raise awareness about these issues, as I firmly believed they warranted a thorough investigation. "The actions of 34x34 cannot be overlooked, and I am committed to ensuring that this situation is addressed appropriately," I stated.

Acknowledging that I should have anticipated the challenges I now face, I made it clear that this would serve as a valuable learning opportunity for MDO Brownie moving forward. The ball was firmly in their court, and I made no attempt to hide my resolve.

The fate of 34x34's employment and the future of the USPS Plantation now rests on how MDO Brownie, Supervisor Purple, and the rest of management choose to respond to my unwavering demands for justice.

CHAPTER 64

Reflection and Action

Dear Lord, why am I going through this? Why did you place me here? What is my purpose in enduring this torment? I try my best to do my job well, but it is only met with unrelenting negativity. I'm growing tired, worn down to my core.

Instead of feeling uplifted when I walk through those doors, I now enter with a sense of dread. Why must I suffer this way? Every time I come to work, rather than finding the support I need, I am only further abused. Dear Lord, what is the reason for putting me in this position?

I've been told that if I don't like it, I should find another job. At first, I considered it, but then I realized, why must I leave when I am doing what is right? Why are those who do wrong allowed to thrive while we who strive for excellence are beaten down?

How can I stand by and watch my fellow coworkers endure the same mistreatment I face and not do anything about it? I cannot accept the injustice, the abuse, the harassment inflicted upon me and so many other hardworking people.

I can't believe they have the audacity to make me feel this way. Who are they to treat me, to treat us with such blatant disrespect? They may not know who I am, but I know who I am. And I am a person who will never give up until what is right is done.

To those who feel as I do, know that you are not alone. I know it feels like the world is against you. I know the union has failed to provide the support you deserve. I know the plant manager and supervisors have turned a blind eye to your struggles.

It has not been easy, I understand. At times, it may feel like you're trapped in a twilight zone, watching as wrong is made to seem right. But it is time for that to change. That is the purpose of this book: to be your platform and your voice.

No matter where you see this book, leave a comment and speak your truth. You must realize that you are not isolated in your suffering. There are many of us going through this at work, but we have been too afraid to come together and speak up.

Well, no more. When we unite and become one voice, our power can no longer be silenced. Join me, and let us rise to shine a light on the abuses we face. It is not fair that we must endure such mistreatment in silence, watching our coworkers be disrespected, abused, and wronged.

The time for silence is over. Speak up, stand up, and fight for the dignity and respect we deserve. This is our workplace, and we will not allow it to be poisoned by those who seek to destroy us. Together, we will forge a new path, one paved with justice, compassion, and the unwavering resolve to create the change we so desperately need.

The future is ours to shape, but only if we have the courage to act. I implore you, my fellow workers, to rise with me and let our voices echo through the halls of this institution, demanding the change that is long overdue.

CHAPTER 65

I'm Going After the Big Dogs

As I continued to endure the relentless injustice and lack of support within the USPS Plantation, I realized that drastic action was essential. If making enough noise was the only way to prompt questions and spark change, then that's exactly what I would do.

When I was called into the general clerk's office, I found myself face to face with Supervisor Miss Island, who had no direct supervisory authority over me. How dare she question me as if I were the aggressor when I was the one who had reported the incident? "Why are you asking me these questions when I'm the victim here?" I demanded, my frustration evident.

Her body language revealed everything I needed to know. Miss Island was fully aware that her actions were wrong, yet she had been chosen to carry out this dirty work, likely to ingratiate herself with the Wolfpack. I left that meeting feeling utterly isolated in my quest for justice, realizing that I would find no support from anyone on this property.

It was time to take matters into my own hands. I composed a pointed email, clearly stating my intention to reach out to the highest levels of the USPS organization. The subject line said it all: "Urgent Concerns Regarding Workplace Injustices."

"My father often advised me that if one is going to raise an issue, it should be done in a way that compels others to take notice and reflect on their actions," I wrote. With this wisdom in mind, I declared my intention to draft a message directly to the USPS Board of Governors and executive team detailing the injustices I had faced at the hands of MDO Brownie and others.

I made it clear that I was seeking a review of the security footage, which could expose how 34x34 had acted without consequence and highlight the incidents involving Rap a Lot and Pat that had been overlooked due to personal connections.

Gothic urged me to pause before sending this email, likely hoping to give MDO Brownie a chance to address these matters appropriately. But I was resolute. "I must emphasize that attempting to protect those in the wrong could lead to serious repercussions for your positions," I warned.

My concern extended beyond my own experience; it was about the integrity of the entire workplace. "I cannot condone the behavior I have endured, including the derogatory remarks made by 34x34," I stated firmly. I demanded fair treatment and set a deadline for them to engage with me on this issue that night. If they failed to respond, I would have no choice but to escalate my concerns and shed light on the mismanagement within USPS Plantation.

“Please understand that I am not one to remain silent in the face of unfair treatment, and I expect acknowledgment of this email,” I wrote. “You should expect calls or messages from corporate following this email if it goes out.”

The ball was now firmly in their court. I had made my demands crystal clear and was prepared to take further action if they did not comply. “Do what is right, or I will have to take the necessary steps to ensure they review the security footage,” I concluded.

True to my word, I informed Gothic that the plant manager, Mr. Gray Suit, would be reaching out to me. And sure enough, the very next day, there he was, approaching me on the platform, his body language betraying his discomfort.

As we walked toward his office, the air was thick with tension. We both knew exactly why we were there, and I was ready to confront him head-on. This was my chance to demand the accountability and justice that had long been denied to me and my fellow coworkers. The time for silence had passed; now, it was time for action.

CHAPTER 66

My Meeting with Mr. Gray Suit

Entering the plant manager's office, I knew this meeting with Mr. Gray Suit would be crucial in my fight for justice. The tension was immediate as we sat facing each other, and I wondered how he'd allowed such workplace toxicity to flourish under his leadership.

I detailed my experiences, 34x34's verbal assaults, Ninja Turtle's attempted physical attack, and Lips' unfounded accusations. Mr. Gray Suit's responses were troublingly dismissive. When I mentioned 34x34's homophobic slurs, he replied callously, "No, it doesn't bother me. Why should it bother you?"

He continued minimizing my experiences, suggesting I shouldn't "react to every single thing" and should just "say something to somebody and expect that they will handle it." His words revealed a disturbing indifference to workplace harassment.

The situation worsened as he diminished the severity of verbal abuse, stating, "She didn't hit you. She didn't go upside your head. She didn't snatch your hat off and say, 'What are you going to do?'", as if only physical violence warranted concern.

Though he claimed he didn't want to "minimize" my feelings, his subsequent remarks only confirmed his profound lack of understanding and empathy. It became clear that the highest authority at USPS Plantation was woefully unequipped to address the systemic issues plaguing our workplace.

Leaving his office, my resolve strengthened. I could no longer depend on this corrupt system for justice. The well-being of all employees hung in the balance, and I was prepared to escalate my fight, regardless of personal consequences. The time for relying on internal channels had ended; now, external action was necessary.

CHAPTER 67

Humpty Dumpty is Being Targeted

After the Ninja Turtle incident, Humpty Dumpty began displaying hostile behavior, giving icy stares, leaving mail behind, and falsely reporting to Supervisor Purple that I hadn't loaded his truck. He'd stand near Slow Mo, a mail handler who could have helped yet always expected me to handle the loading.

His intimidation tactics escalated to loud conversations with Pastor and 3434, shouting to Ninja Turtle, "WE MISS YOU, GIRL!" But at 6'3" and 210 pounds, I wasn't easily frightened by words. When alone, his bravado disappeared; he'd rush from the truck without his cheering squad. Eventually, I confronted him, explaining he had no real grievance with me. Surprisingly, we became cordial afterward.

The dynamics shifted when Humpty Dumpty feuded with Dust Cuz, revealing workplace politics at their worst. Dust Cuz, seeking revenge, ordered me to move mail loading from the efficient doors 15-16 to door 22, creating unnecessary work and confusion. When I questioned this illogical change, he admitted wanting to "teach Humpty Dumpty a lesson."

I refused to participate in this petty vendetta. The situation worsened when Dust Cuz began poisoning others against Humpty Dumpty, particularly influencing Expediter Light Skin's treatment of him. Witnessing this toxicity, I chose to show Humpty Dumpty extra kindness, recognizing the broader issue of workplace bullying at USPS Plantation.

Though Dust Cuz and Humpty Dumpty eventually reconciled, the incident exposed a darker truth: sometimes those we consider friends actively work to undermine us. This experience reinforced my belief that we must speak against injustice, whether it affects us directly or not. Not everyone has the strength to defend themselves, and those who can speak up have a responsibility to do so.

The irony lies in their current friendly relationship, with Humpty Dumpty unaware of Dust Cuz's previous betrayal. It's a stark reminder that workplace relationships often mask hidden agendas, and those smiling in your face might be orchestrating your difficulties behind the scenes.

CHAPTER 68

A Total Injustice I've Been Served

Dear Lord, why this injustice? I followed every rule, yet I'm being punished as if I were the wrongdoer. The plant manager, Mr. Gray Suit, told me to "say something to somebody and expect that they will handle it." I did exactly that, but the system failed me.

When a USPS-appointed lead approached Gothic and me disrespectfully, I calmly sought clarification about her behavior. Her response was immediate and vicious: "I knew you were going to bring your bitch ass over here with that gay shit. Stop acting like a faggot. Be a man, faggot." While her crew of six to eight people laughed, I simply raised my hands, said, "Okay," and sought a supervisor to report the incident.

Despite following protocol and informing supervisors, the union, and plant management, I received a seven-day in-house suspension. When I discussed this with

Sweaty Eyes, the union president, he, like with the Lips incident, shifted the blame onto me.

The absurdity deepens. 34X34, a known lesbian, attacks me with homophobic slurs, yet Sweaty Eyes fixates on my comment about her wanting to be a man. My point was simple: true manhood means showing restraint and respect, not aggression. Had a man approached me with such slurs, the confrontation would've ended differently.

Watching Cushion's expression during my meeting with Sweaty Eyes confirmed the obvious injustice. I left determined to reform this broken union system. When someone follows every rule yet faces punishment while their abuser goes free, what options remain? This systematic failure drives people to snap and go postal. That's why I wrote "The Journey of a Postal Employee: Going Postal."

CHAPTER 69

My Final Cry

As I reflect on the turmoil of the past few weeks, I can't help but feel the weight of a system that has failed me. The frustration, the anger, the helplessness, it all boils over within me, leaving me questioning everything I thought I knew about justice and fairness in the workplace.

How is it that I did everything right, only to be treated like the wrongdoer? It's a bitter pill to swallow. Workplace abuse is not just a personal experience; it's a reality for many employees across various industries. The psychological toll it takes can be devastating; stress, anxiety, depression, and even PTSD can manifest in those who are subjected to relentless mistreatment. We've all heard the stories, the tragic headlines of employees pushed to their limits, resorting to violence in a desperate cry for help. It's frightening to think about, but it's a reality we cannot ignore.

The USPS has not been immune to these incidents. There are reports of shootings aimed at supervisors and management, highlighting the extreme reactions that can stem from an environment of fear, abuse, and neglect. Employees who feel undervalued, disrespected, and unheard can find themselves at a breaking point, where the line between right and wrong blurs. It's a chilling reminder of what can happen when the scales of justice tip too far, leaving individuals feeling powerless and desperate.

I am not advocating for violence; I never will. However, I understand the pain and frustration that can build up in an environment that fosters abuse and neglect. The reality is that you could be just one incident away from snapping, one moment that sends you over the edge. It's easy to say that violence is never the answer, but when the system fails to protect you and holds you accountable for the actions of others, it can feel like there are no other options left.

I think of the countless employees who have suffered in silence, who have felt the sting of verbal abuse, the weight of emotional distress, and the crushing blow of being unjustly reprimanded. They are left to navigate their pain alone, often feeling that speaking up will only bring more retribution. It's a cycle that perpetuates itself, leaving a trail of broken spirits and shattered lives.

As I sit here, I vow to channel my frustration into something constructive. I refuse to let the injustices I've faced define me or push me into a corner. Instead, I will use my voice to advocate for change and raise awareness about the importance of addressing workplace abuse before it escalates into something far worse. I will stand up for those who cannot stand up for themselves, pushing for policy changes and a culture of respect and accountability within the USPS.

The story of one employee may seem small in the grand scheme of things, but it can spark a movement. It's time for us to come together and demand a workplace where respect prevails and where employees feel safe to express their concerns without fear of reprisal. We need to ensure that no one else feels the need to go postal to resort to violence because they feel cornered and unheard.

As I close this chapter of my journey, I do so with a renewed sense of purpose. I will not be silenced. I will not back down. It's time to rewrite the narrative, not just for myself but for every employee who has ever felt the sting of injustice. Together, we can foster a work environment that values humanity over hierarchy, prioritizes respect over retaliation, and believes in the collective power of its workforce.

The road ahead may be long and fraught with challenges, but I am determined to be a catalyst for change. And if that means shaking the very foundations of the USPS, then so be it. Because, in the end, it's about more than just me; it's about creating a brighter future for all of us.

CHAPTER 70

My Letter To USPS

Dear USPS Leaders and USPS Mail Handler Union, I come to you today with a sincere plea for help, hoping my voice will be heard amidst the noise. As a dedicated employee for the past four years, I find myself in a workplace that has become synonymous with disorganization and abuse. It's disheartening to realize that in a federal government job, I would encounter such distressing circumstances. Many of us are suffering quietly, yearning for change and support, only to feel abandoned in our struggles.

While we have a union that is meant to advocate for us, it seems the system is failing to provide the adequate support we desperately need. I've taken the initiative to research the alarming incidents of employees who have been pushed to their breaking points, and it's a painful reflection of our reality. We cannot afford to remain oblivious to the cries of our colleagues who suffer under the leadership you have placed in power to guide and protect us.

I believe that our management team and union representatives need to prioritize the mental health and well-being of all employees. Too many incidents have gone unaddressed, leaving us feeling unheard and vulnerable in our work environment. We are simply asking for a safe space to work, one free from harassment, bullying, and trauma. The management and supervisors in leadership roles need immediate retraining; many are unfit to guide us.

One of the critical issues we face is the lack of effective union representation. How can a union representative truly advocate for us when they are juggling operational duties and lack the time needed to thoroughly investigate employee concerns? I have witnessed firsthand union representatives rushing back to their tasks, leaving critical issues unresolved. Furthermore, if they are still part of the facility, they may be subjected to the same management pressures and bullying, which compromises their ability to represent us effectively.

I propose that we bring in outside union representatives, individuals who are not affiliated with our building and can focus solely on union-related tasks. This change is vital; we need representatives who are free from the influence of management and who can genuinely advocate for our rights without fear of retaliation or bias.

It is disheartening to see resources wasted on trivial items, aprons, pens, and bags, while we lack the essential support we truly need. The money spent should be invested in ensuring we have well-trained representatives who can navigate our concerns with expertise and compassion. Many of us feel like our cases are stuck in limbo, with no clear path forward, because we lack proper representation.

We must hold ourselves accountable and demand better from our leadership. The toxic environment that many of us endure is unacceptable. It's time for higher-ups to recognize that a company is only as strong as its employees, and when we are treated poorly, it becomes difficult for us to excel. While we hear about the pride in our work, I find it hard to feel that pride when our workplace is mired in dysfunction.

We all deserve to come to work each day and focus on our tasks without the shadow of abuse or harassment looming over us. Work-life balance is crucial, and right now, it feels severely off-kilter. Let's unite in our call for change and hold management and the union accountable for creating an environment where we can thrive. Together, we can foster a workplace that reflects the values we all aspire to uphold.

Thank you for your time and consideration. Let's work together to create a better future for all of us at USPS.

Sincerely,

Sir Francis T. Blackwood

CHAPTER 71

My Final Plea For Change

As I reflect the tumultuous journey I've endured at the USPS Plantation, a deep sorrow weighs heavily on my heart. The abuse, the harassment, and the utter lack of respect and support have taken an irreparable toll on my mental and emotional well-being.

Day after day, I walk through those doors, bracing myself for the relentless mistreatment that awaits. The disorganization and blatant disregard for our welfare are enough to push anyone to the brink of despair. And yet, when I reach out for help and plead for the protection I so rightfully deserve, I am met with indifference, a callous dismissal of my cries.

That is why I have documented each and every incident and created an irrefutable paper trail demanding attention and action. Still, my pleas for justice have fallen on deaf ears.

I find myself asking: What have I done to deserve such torment? Why must I, and so many of my colleagues, suffer in silence while those entrusted to lead us remain complicit in our anguish? The injustice of it all is enough to make my blood boil.

As I reflect the tragic incidents of postal shootings, I can't help but feel a deep empathy for those who have been pushed to the edge. For the families of those who lost their lives, the pain they must endure is unimaginable. When the weight of abuse becomes too much to bear, when the system fails us time and time again, what other recourse do we have? This is not an excuse but a plea for understanding, an acknowledgment that we are all human, and even the strongest can be broken.

I want this book to be a clarion call, a demand for accountability and change. I want the powers that be to look deep within and ask, "How have we allowed this to happen?" I want them to see the faces of the broken, the traumatized, the desperate and to feel the weight of their inaction.

This is why I have provided the Workplace Abuse Documentation Chart, a tool to empower employees like myself to systematically record the incidents of abuse we face. With this evidence in hand, we can no longer be ignored, dismissed, or silenced. It is time for the USPS to address the toxic culture that has taken root.

This is not just my story; it is the story of countless employees who failed by a system meant to protect us. We deserve better. We deserve a workplace where respect, dignity, and compassion are the cornerstones, not a breeding ground for abuse and neglect.

So, I implore you, those in power, those who hold our livelihoods in your hands, listen to our cries, feel the pain in our words, and take the necessary steps to enact the change we so desperately need. For if you fail us once more, the consequences may be unimaginable. If another postal employee is pushed to the brink due to management's abuse, the USPS must be held accountable for any loss of life. We should no longer ignore the employees who are mistreated every day and use mental illness as an excuse to overlook the toxic workplace that is allowed to fester.

This is my final plea, my last desperate attempt to be heard. I refuse to be silenced or broken. Together, we will rise from the ashes of this toxic environment and forge a new path, one paved with the respect and support we rightfully deserve. The time for change is now.

CHAPTER 72

UPDATE As Of March 13, 2025

The past few years have been a journey filled with challenges, and 2024 proved particularly overwhelming. My personal life became chaotic, and just before Christmas, I received the devastating news that a close family member had been diagnosed with cancer. In that moment, I found myself questioning God: Why me? Haven't I endured enough? During this dark time, I recalled the words of 1 Corinthians 10:13: "No temptation has overtaken you except what is common to mankind. And God is faithful; he will not let you be tempted beyond what you can bear. But when you are tempted, he will also provide a way out so that you can endure it." This promise became my anchor, reminding me that the Lord would not give me more than I could handle. I leaned on Him more than ever.

I prayed earnestly, hoping that 2024 would be the most challenging year I would face and that brighter days would follow in 2025. Renewing my faith in God, I felt immense gratitude when my family member's surgery was successful. Thank you, Lord, for your protection.

This cancer scare prompted deep reflection and rekindled my commitment to making a positive impact at USPS. I believe God placed this challenge before me because He trusts me to help transform the toxic and abusive culture there. His assurance that I wouldn't face more than I could bear resonated deeply within me.

I am delighted to share that Supervisor Purple is no longer with the platform. We have welcomed a new supervisor whose first words to me were, "I hope you won't give me any problems." I laughed, feeling no urge to defend myself against assumptions based on rumors. Within two weeks, she recognized Gothic and me as the go-to people for getting work done, treating us far better than Purple ever did.

The new supervisor also addressed the poor leadership of 34X34, confronting her about her frequent absences from the platform when there's work to be done and even having to clock her out due to her disappearances. This was a relief, as 34X34 has been shirking responsibilities for years, often sleeping on the job and contributing nothing during her regular work hours and when she's here working overtime. Our new supervisor offered Gothic and me the opportunity to transfer to the line operation, and after careful consideration, we accepted. She is by far the best supervisor we've had, even promoting us from level 4 to level 5, which comes with a pay raise. The line is less stressful and keeps us away from the platform drama.

Unfortunately, I don't have positive updates regarding 34X34. She continues to sleep at work. To those in USPS corporate reading this, I urge you to investigate her. Review the camera footage, and you'll see that she contributes nothing all night. I still wonder who she is related to, as her behavior is continually overlooked by management.

As for Ninja Turtle, Slow Mo (aka Turtle), Carmen Sandiego, and Pastor, there are no positive changes to report, and they persist in their old ways.

On a brighter note, I'm thrilled to announce that Gothic has decided to return to school. She's enrolled in a university, studying Information Technology with a focus on Cybersecurity. I am incredibly proud of her, especially as she made the Dean's List last semester with a 4.0 GPA. Sometimes, life's challenges remind us that we can do better and deserve more. I believe her journey at USPS opened her eyes and inspired her to strive for greater achievements.

As for me, while writing this book, I realized I needed to speak to someone about my mental health. I reached out to USPS EAP (www.EAP4YOU or call 1-800-327-4968). Reflecting on these traumatic incidents made me realize the extent of the abuse and harassment I've faced, and I needed someone to help me navigate the built-up resentment towards management. I am also grateful to start a new chapter of my life as an author. Sometimes, it is through our lowest moments that we truly discover our resilience. I have battled with ADHD for years, often struggling to start and complete tasks. I am proud to say that if you are reading this right now, it means I was able to fight my ADHD and finish this book, "The Journey of a Postal Employee: Going Postal."

I am uncertain about what will happen when I release this book, but I pray it makes enough of an impact that the USPS leadership takes notice and implements necessary changes to improve morale and address the toxic environment. I also understand that I might not have a job after this book comes out, but I am willing to take that risk to create a better work environment for all USPS employees.

To anyone reading this and feeling alone or uncertain, I want you to know that you are not alone. I invite you to join me in stopping the abuse taking place at your job. Wherever you see this book or anything related, I encourage you to share your experiences. Let's build a community around ourselves and advocate for change. You can also reach out to me at Goingpostalbook@gmail.com. If you want to support me in my next book project, please feel free to Cash App me at $FTN1211.

I truly appreciate you for reading my book. Always remember: Dream + Passion + Drive = SUCCESS. Stay blessed.

CHAPTER 73

Final Chapter

I thought my journey had reached its conclusion, but it seems I was mistaken. Recently, I was summoned to the general clerk's office by the new supervisor, whom I've nicknamed Owl. To my shock, I was handed a 14-day suspension for attendance issues. Confusion washed over me—I had never received any verbal or written warnings about my attendance. When I inquired about the reason for this suspension, Owl informed me that it was the directive from our labor union. I turned to Union Rep Cushion for clarification, only to learn that such a suspension was not standard procedure.

Owl claimed my suspension stemmed from a prior seven-day in-house suspension, which had been issued after I reported 34X34 for using homophobic slurs against me. I brought up the grievance I had requested Cushion and Union President Sweaty Eyes to file regarding the seven-day suspension. Despite my efforts to follow proper channels, the lack of communication and resolution regarding my situation has been frustrating.

Email to Management:

Good afternoon,

I feel compelled to share a deeply troubling experience that I have faced within our workplace.

I was subjected to homophobic remarks by my team lead, a situation that I believe all of you are aware of. Following this incident, I received a seven-day in-house suspension, which prompted me to reach out to our Union Representative, Cushion. I even went to the office to speak with the Union President, Mr. Sweaty Eyes, about filing a grievance regarding this matter.

Unfortunately, I have encountered ongoing frustration with the back-and-forth communication between the union and management. Despite my efforts to stay informed, including reaching out to everyone involved and sending numerous emails, it seems no one has clear answers about the status of my grievance. This lack of resolution has left a mark on my record and has contributed to the 14-day suspension I was recently informed about by Owl.

I am formally requesting that this unjust 14-day suspension be addressed through the grievance process, as Cushion has indicated she would. However, when I inquired about updates, I was told that my grievance had been submitted to my supervisor for review. When I approached Owl regarding this, she claimed to have received no paperwork or communication from Cushion regarding my case.

It feels as though my concerns continually fall into a void—unresolved and without recourse. I am documenting this situation not only for my own records but also to express my frustration at the apparent lack of support from the union. Why do I feel targeted? Why is my representation falling short?

I urge everyone involved to take a moment to reflect on the importance of standing up for what is right. You may not have to like me, but I implore you to fulfill your responsibilities with integrity, just as I strive to do my job to the best of my ability within this facility.

Thank you for your attention to this matter. I sincerely hope for a resolution that reflects fairness and justice.

Sincerely,

Sir Francis T. Blackwood

I want to clarify that while some may believe I am unaffected by the ongoing issues I've encountered, the reality is quite different. I have been meticulously documenting every instance of abuse and have communicated with various individuals in management to establish a clear paper trail.

I look forward to the release of my project next month, which will shed light on these matters. I have addressed my concerns with management, yet they have chosen to overlook the issues I've raised.

I want to emphasize that I am not like many others here at the USPS Plantation; I possess a level of insight and intelligence that may not be fully recognized.

I hope this message finds you well. I am reaching out to express my concerns regarding the representation I have received from the union. Over the past three years, I have communicated via email about the unfair treatment I have experienced, yet I feel that I have not received the adequate support I need during my cases. I have documentation, including emails and text messages, that demonstrate my ongoing struggles and the lack of assistance from the union in addressing these issues. While I understand that there may be personal feelings involved, I believe it is essential for the union to fulfill its primary role of protecting the rights of workers. Unfortunately, I have not witnessed this support concerning my cases. Currently, I am facing a potential suspension due to attendance issues, despite not having received any verbal warnings. I am documenting this situation for my records, as I feel it is important to have a paper trail. Additionally, I would like to formally file another grievance. The previous grievance concerning inappropriate remarks made by a team lead has remained unresolved for over five months, despite my repeated inquiries. I am addressing this message directly to you as the union president, with the hope that you will take my cases seriously. It is important for me to communicate how I have felt unsupported throughout this process, and I believe that transparency is crucial. I encourage you to investigate these matters further, as I will be sharing my experiences with my colleagues. Thank you for your attention to these issues. I look forward to your response.

Sincerely,

Sir Francis T. Blackwood

I must also mention that, as I had predicted, Gothic and I were moved to the B section of the platform. We were promised level 5 pay while we worked at the line operation. It has now been almost a month of working in the line operation, and we still haven't received our level 5 pay. When we asked about it, we were given the usual excuses. It's frustrating how there are always excuses when it comes to Gothic and me. Meanwhile, some former drivers are still receiving level 5 pay.

This situation feels all too familiar, reminiscent of what happened to Supervisor Purple. Supervisor Owl is starting to show signs of weakness, likely influenced by 34X34 and her crew. They've managed to call off and frustrate Supervisor Owl to the point where she's behaving differently— laughing and joking with them. She even complained to MDO Brownie about 34X34, only to be told to ignore her. It seems clear to me that 34X34 must be related to MDO Brownie.

I was informed by Union Rep Cushion that Brownie was the reason behind my seven-day in-house suspension. It appears she is deliberately targeting supervisors to ensure I receive harsher treatment. It baffles me how she can expect Supervisor Owl to let 34X34 off the hook when Owl wants to discipline her. All the while, the best workers are subjected to the harshest treatment. I genuinely believe MDO Brownie should be demoted; she's not making decisions that benefit our facility.

Furthermore, I suspect that some of the managements are receiving pay without being physically present on the property. I have my reasons for saying this; it seems like many of them are absent, and whenever something goes wrong, I hear supervisors calling them, and they always sound as if they've just woken up. It's concerning that we barely see MDO Brownie around, while MDO Brother Man and the African Male MDO are more frequently visible. I suspect a few MDOs are on the payroll without actually doing the work. If you don't believe me, conduct an investigation. There's nothing to lose and a lot to gain when you uncover the truth behind these issues.

So, here I am, still fighting against mistreatment without true support. This is not right. We need new management or a retraining of the ones we have. Good workers should not continue to be mistreated or feel isolated in their struggles.

CHAPTER 74

Workplace Abuse Documentation and Employee Empowerment

In the ongoing fight against workplace abuse and injustice, documentation is a powerful tool that can help drive meaningful change. By equipping employees with a structured approach to recording incidents, we empower them to take an active role in addressing the issues they face.

Introducing the Workplace Abuse Documentation Chart:

This interactive chart provides a comprehensive framework for employees to document their experiences of abuse, discrimination, and unfair treatment in the workplace. By filling out this form, employees can create a clear, detailed record that can be used to support their claims and initiate the necessary actions for resolution.

How to Use the Chart:

1. Employee Information: Fill in your name and the date of the incident.
2. Incident Details: Record the time and location where the abuse occurred.
3. Type of Abuse: Check all the boxes that apply to the type of abuse you experienced, from verbal and emotional to discrimination and retaliation.
4. Detailed Description: Provide a thorough account of the incident, including any relevant context or details.
5. Witnesses: List the names and contact information of any individuals who witnessed the event.
6. Actions Taken: Document any steps you have taken, such as reporting the incident to a supervisor or filing a formal complaint.
7. Outcome: If you are aware of the outcome or resolution of the incident, please note it here.
8. Employee Signature: Sign the form to validate the information provided.

Empowering Employees, Driving Change:

By using this Workplace Abuse Documentation Chart, employees can take a proactive stance in addressing the issues they face. The structured format ensures that critical details are captured, creating a robust paper trail that can be used to support their claims and advocate for change.

Moreover, the act of documenting these incidents can be a powerful step in itself, as it reinforces the employee's right to a safe and respectful work environment. It demonstrates a commitment to holding the organization accountable and a refusal to be silenced.

Join the Movement for Workplace Justice:

We encourage all employees who have experienced or witnessed workplace abuse to utilize this Workplace Abuse Documentation Chart. By sharing your stories and submitting your completed forms, you can contribute to a growing database of evidence that will help drive systemic change within the USPS and beyond.

Together, we can create a future where respect, dignity, and fairness are the cornerstones of every workplace. Let's stand united, raise our voices, and demand the change that is long overdue.

Workplace Abuse Documentation Chart

Employee Name: ______________________________
Date: ___/___/_____
Time of Incident: _____ : _____ AM / PM
Location of Incident: ______________________________

Type of Abuse *(check all that apply)*:

☐ Verbal Abuse (e.g., yelling, insults)
☐ Emotional Abuse (e.g., humiliation, isolation)
☐ Discrimination (e.g., based on race, gender)
☐ Harassment (e.g., unwanted physical contact)
☐ Unreasonable Demands (e.g., excessive workload)
☐ Retaliation (e.g., punishment for reporting)
☐ Other: ______________________________

Detailed Description of Incident:

____

____

____

____

Witnesses (if any):

1. **Name:** ______________________________
   Contact Info: ______________________________
2. **Name:** ______________________________
   Contact Info: ______________________________

Actions Taken *(e.g., reported to a supervisor)*:

____

____

____

Outcome *(if known)*:

____

____

____

Employee Signature: ______________________________

This template includes the essential information needed to document workplace abuse, such as the date, time, location, type of abuse, a detailed description of the incident, any witness, and the actions taken. It also provides space for the employee to describe the outcome, if known.

Encouraging employees to use a standardized form like this can help them systematically record incidents, which can be crucial evidence if further action is required. It's important for employees to document abuse as soon as possible while the details are fresh in their memory. We are all in this together.

Chart 1: General Workplace Abuse Report Form

Employee Name: ____________________________
Date: ____ / ____ / ______
Time of Incident: ______ : ______ AM / PM
Location of Incident: ____________________________

Type of Abuse (check all that apply):
☐ Verbal Abuse ☐ Emotional Abuse ☐ Discrimination ☐ Harassment
☐ Unreasonable Demands ☐ Retaliation ☐ Other: ________________________

Detailed Description of Incident:

Immediate Action Taken:

Witnesses (Name & Contact):

1. ______________________ ______________________
2. ______________________ ______________________

Employee Signature: ____________________________

Chart 2: Managerial Misconduct Incident Report

Employee Name: ______________________________
Manager/Supervisor Involved: ______________________________
Date/Time of Incident: ______________________________
Location: ______________________________

Nature of Misconduct:
☐ Abusive Language ☐ Favoritism ☐ Disciplinary Threats
☐ Denial of Breaks ☐ Unjustified Write-up ☐ Public Shaming
☐ Other: ______________________________

Summary of What Occurred:

How the Incident Affected You (emotionally or physically)?

Any Prior Incidents with Same Manager?
☐ Yes ☐ No If Yes, Date(s): ______________________________

Reported To (if applicable): ______________________________
Employee Signature: ______________________________

Chart 3: Peer-to-Peer Conflict Report

Employee Name: ______________________________
Other Party Involved: ______________________________
Date: ____ / ____ / ______
Time: ______ : ______ AM / PM
Location of Incident: ______________________________

Type of Incident (check all that apply):
☐ Disrespectful Behavior ☐ Gossip/Slander ☐ Threats
☐ Harassment ☐ Physical Intimidation ☐ Social Exclusion

Description of Interaction:

Attempts Made to Resolve Conflict:
☐ Conversation ☐ Mediation ☐ Supervisor Notified ☐ None

Desired Outcome:

Employee Signature: ______________________________

Chart 3: Peer-to-Peer Conflict Report

Employee Name: ______________________________
Other Party Involved: ______________________________
Date: ____ / ____ / ______
Time: ______ : ______ AM / PM
Location of Incident: ______________________________

Type of Incident (check all that apply):

☐ **Disrespectful Behavior** ☐ **Gossip/Slander** ☐ **Threats**

☐ **Harassment** ☐ **Physical Intimidation** ☐ **Social Exclusion**

Description of Interaction:

Attempts Made to Resolve Conflict:

☐ **Conversation** ☐ **Mediation** ☐ **Supervisor Notified** ☐ **None**

Desired Outcome:

Employee Signature: ______________________________

Chart 4: Witness Statement Form

Witness Name: ______________________________
Contact Info: ______________________________
Date of Incident: ____ / ____ / ______
Time: ______ : ______ AM / PM
Location: ______________________________

Person(s) Involved: ______________________________
Type of Abuse Witnessed:
☐ Verbal ☐ Emotional ☐ Discrimination ☐ Harassment ☐ Retaliation

What Did You Witness? (Be specific):

How Did You Respond (if at all)?

Additional Notes or Concerns:

Signature of Witness: ______________________________

Chart 5: Follow-Up and Resolution Tracker

Employee Name: ______________________________
Original Incident Report Date: ____ / ____ / ______
Date of Follow-Up: ____ / ____ / ______

Was the Incident Acknowledged by Management?
☐ Yes ☐ No Date: ______________________________

Investigation Status:
☐ Ongoing ☐ Resolved ☐ Dismissed ☐ Escalated

Resolution Steps Taken:
☐ Verbal Warning Issued
☐ Written Warning
☐ Mediation Conducted
☐ Transfer/Separation
☐ Other: ______________________________

Employee Satisfaction with Outcome:
☐ Satisfied ☐ Partially Satisfied ☐ Not Satisfied

Comments:

Employee Signature: ______________________________

Chart 6: Anonymous Report Slip

Date: ___ / ___ / ____

Department: ______________________

Type of Abuse:

☐ Verbal ☐ Emotional ☐ Harassment ☐ Retaliation

☐ Discrimination ☐ Other: ______________________

Brief Description:

Still Ongoing? ☐ Yes ☐ No

Optional Contact (if follow-up desired): ______________________

Chart 7: Sexual Harassment Complaint Form

Employee Name: ________________________

Date/Time: ___ / ___ / _____ _____ : _____ AM / PM

Location: ________________________

Accused Individual: ________________________

Incident Details:

Witnesses (if any):

Impact (emotional/psychological/physical):

Desired Action:

☐ Investigation ☐ Apology ☐ Transfer ☐ Other: ________________________

Employee Signature: ________________________

Chart 8: Physical Intimidation Report

Employee Name: ______________________

Offender's Name: ______________________

Date/Time: ___ / ___ / _____ _____ : _____ AM / PM

Location: ______________________

Describe the Intimidating Behavior:

☐ Pacing ☐ Blocking Paths ☐ Aggressive Gestures ☐ Threats

Any Physical Contact? ☐ Yes ☐ No

Security or HR Notified? ☐ Yes ☐ No

Action Taken (if any):

Employee Signature: ______________________

Chart 9: Emotional Distress Journal

Name (Optional): ________________________

Date of Entry: ___ / ___ / _____

Incident or Triggering Event:

Emotional Response:

☐ Anxiety ☐ Panic ☐ Depression ☐ Frustration

Duration of Distress: ________________________

Support Accessed:

☐ None ☐ Counselor ☐ Supervisor ☐ HR

Notes:

Chart 10: Retaliation Monitoring Log

Employee Name: ________________________

Original Complaint Date: ___/___/_____

Retaliation Date: ___/___/_____

Type of Retaliation (check all that apply):

☐ Shift Reduction ☐ Isolation ☐ Write-Up

☐ Denied Opportunities ☐ Hostility ☐ Other: ________________________

Describe What Happened:

Witnesses:

Reported To: ________________________

Chart 11: Management Response Record

Manager Name: ________________________

Employee Concern Raised: ________________________

Date Received: ___/___/____

Meeting Held? ☐ Yes ☐ No Date: ________________________

Manager's Actions:

☐ Acknowledged Complaint

☐ Opened Investigation

☐ Deferred/Delayed Action

☐ Dismissed Concern

☐ Other: ________________________

Notes:

Manager Signature: ________________________

Chart 12: Confidential Mediation Request

Employee Requesting: ________________________

Other Party Involved: ________________________

Date of Request: ___/___/_____

Nature of Dispute:

☐ Harassment ☐ Miscommunication ☐ Disrespect

☐ Personality Conflict ☐ Other: ________________________

Preferred Mediation Format:

☐ In-Person ☐ Virtual ☐ Group Setting

Goal for Mediation:

Chart 13: Burnout & Overload Report

Employee Name: ________________________

Department: ________________________

Date: ___ / ___ / ____

Symptoms of Burnout:

☐ Fatigue ☐ Irritability ☐ Low Motivation

☐ Absenteeism ☐ Isolation ☐ Other: ________________________

Cause of Stress (if known):

☐ Excessive Workload ☐ Hostile Environment

☐ Poor Leadership ☐ Lack of Resources

What Support Is Needed?

Signature (Optional): ________________________

Chart 14: Abuse Incident Timeline

Date	Type of Abuse	Perpetrator	Reported?	Action Taken
			☐ Yes ☐ No	
			☐ Yes ☐ No	
			☐ Yes ☐ No	

Chart 15: Supervisor Misconduct Pattern Log

Supervisor Name: ________________________

Employee Submitting: ________________________

Start Date: ___/___/____

End Date (if applicable): ___/___/____

Incident Descriptions (Use new row for each):

Date	Misconduct Type	Description	Witnesses	Reported?
				☐ Yes ☐ No
				☐ Yes ☐ No

Chart 16: Workplace Culture Feedback Survey

(Anonymous — Optional Contact Info)
Date: ____ / ____ / ______

Please rate the following statements:
(1 = Strongly Disagree, 5 = Strongly Agree)

- I feel safe in my work environment. 1 2 3 4 5
- Management handles complaints fairly. 1 2 3 4 5
- I can report abuse without fear of retaliation. 1 2 3 4 5
- Bullying and harassment are addressed promptly. 1 2 3 4 5

Have you personally experienced or witnessed abuse?
☐ Yes ☐ No If Yes, briefly describe:

Suggestions for Improvement:

Optional Contact Info: ______________________________

Chart 17: Group Incident Report

Team/Department: ______________________________
Date of Incident: ____ / ____ / ______
Time: ______ : ______ AM / PM
Location: ______________________________

People Involved:

1. ____
2. ____
3. ____

Nature of Incident (check all that apply):

☐ Verbal Altercation ☐ Managerial Abuse
☐ Unsafe Behavior ☐ Hostile Environment
☐ Policy Violation ☐ Other: ______________________________

Group Description of Incident:

____

Team Action Taken (if any):

____

Group Representative Signature: ______________________________

Chart 18: Remote Work Abuse Log

Employee Name: ______________________________
Date: ____ / ____ / ______
Platform Used: ☐ Zoom ☐ Teams ☐ Slack ☐ Email ☐ Other: __________

Type of Abuse Experienced Remotely:

☐ Inappropriate Messages
☐ Constant Micromanagement
☐ Exclusion from Meetings
☐ Hostile Tone or Threats
☐ Other: ______________________________

Description with Timestamps or Evidence:

Reported To: ______________________________
Follow-Up Received?: ☐ Yes ☐ No

Chart 19: Third-Party Abuse Report

Employee Name: ______________________________
Third Party (Customer/Vendor/Contractor): ______________________________
Date/Time of Incident: ______________________________
Location/Platform: ______________________________

Type of Abuse:
☐ Verbal ☐ Sexual Harassment ☐ Threats ☐ Discrimination
☐ Refusal to Respect Boundaries ☐ Other: ______________________________

Description of What Occurred:

Reported To Supervisor/HR?: ☐ Yes ☐ No
Action Requested:
☐ Ban/Restrict Access
☐ Formal Complaint to Vendor/Agency
☐ Other: ______________________________

Chart 20: Whistleblower Protection Form

Employee Name: ____________________________
Date: ____ / ____ / ______
Department: ____________________________

What are you reporting?

☐ Policy Violation ☐ Safety Issue ☐ Abuse or Harassment
☐ Ethical Breach ☐ Fraud/Corruption ☐ Retaliation

Detailed Report (Include names, dates, evidence):

Do you wish to remain anonymous? ☐ Yes ☐ No
Are you experiencing retaliation as a result of this report? ☐ Yes ☐ No

Contact (optional for follow-up): ____________________________

www.ingramcontent.com/pod-product-compliance
Lightning Source LLC
LaVergne TN
LVHW080044210926
848481LV00011B/3278